Cambridge Elements ≡

Elements in Theatre, Performance and the Political
edited by
Trish Reid
University of Reading
Liz Tomlin
University of Glasgow

DECOLONISING AFRICAN THEATRE

Samuel Ravengai
University of the Witwatersrand

CAMBRIDGE
UNIVERSITY PRESS

Shaftesbury Road, Cambridge CB2 8EA, United Kingdom

One Liberty Plaza, 20th Floor, New York, NY 10006, USA

477 Williamstown Road, Port Melbourne, VIC 3207, Australia

314–321, 3rd Floor, Plot 3, Splendor Forum, Jasola District Centre, New Delhi – 110025, India

103 Penang Road, #05–06/07, Visioncrest Commercial, Singapore 238467

Cambridge University Press is part of Cambridge University Press & Assessment, a department of the University of Cambridge.

We share the University's mission to contribute to society through the pursuit of education, learning and research at the highest international levels of excellence.

www.cambridge.org
Information on this title: www.cambridge.org/9781009500449

DOI: 10.1017/9781009271455

First published 2024

A catalogue record for this publication is available from the British Library.

ISBN 978-1-009-50044-9 Hardback
ISBN 978-1-009-27147-9 Paperback
ISSN 2753-1244 (online)
ISSN 2753-1236 (print)

Decolonising African Theatre

Elements in Theatre, Performance and the Political

DOI: 10.1017/9781009271455
First published online: March 2024

Samuel Ravengai
University of the Witwatersrand

Author for correspondence: Samuel Ravengai, Samuel.Ravengai@wits.ac.za

Abstract: Decolonisation can be pursued in different ways. After many years of developing a critical language to engage coloniality, the most urgent need in African theatre is to develop new theories and methods in our manufactories. This Element uses Afroscenology as a theory to read and comment on African theatre. The Element particularly focuses on the history of laboratories in which it was tested and emerged, the historicisation of rombic theatre and the crafting of a theory of the playtext which has been named theatric theory to distinguish it from the Aristotelian dramatic theory. The second dimension of the theory is the performatic technique. This Element also explains Afrosonic mime through examples drawn from the workshops conducted in training performers.

Keywords: Afroscenology, dariro/canto, rombic theatre, decolonisation, Afrosonic mime

ISBNs: 9781009500449 (HB), 9781009271479 (PB), 9781009271455 (OC)
ISSNs: 2753-1244 (online), 2753-1236 (print)

Contents

1 Introduction: Canonising an African Theory of Theatre   1

2 Reconfiguring African Theatre Episteme: Formulating
   the Theory of Afroscenology   17

3 Rombic Theatre: Celebrating the Fools
   of Africa and Crafting a Theory   31

4 Afrosonic Mime: A Post-psychophysical Perspective   47

5 Conclusion   61

References   68

1 Introduction: Canonising an African Theory of Theatre

This Element sets out to formulate an African theory of African theatre. While the size and diversity of the continent make generating a comprehensive conceptual framework challenging, research has shown that Africans – including those in the diaspora – responded to colonial presence and white supremacism in specific and quantifiable creative ways (Mbembe, 2017; Taylor, 2016). More specifically, in the postcolonial period, African artist-researchers developed a repertoire of plays variously called the 'great tradition', the 'African canon', or 'art theatre', which encodes modes of writing and performance quite distinct from western traditions (Etherton, 1982). Within this tradition, two strands emerged – African epic theatre and what I have chosen to call *rombic* theatre (as distinct from *avant garde* theatre). The African great tradition has been largely neglected in scholarship and, where it has been analysed, inappropriate theories have been applied leading to misleading conclusions. This Element propounds a new theory – Afroscenology – adequate to a fuller appreciation of these works. In so doing, it challenges the dominance of western epistemologies in the field of theatre and performance studies and expands the critical vocabulary available to scholars in the discipline. It is not intended as a comprehensive, all-encompassing, or orthodox theory, to which other scholars and/or practitioners should defer. Instead, the hope is that it will challenge others to develop new theoretical approaches for the appreciation of decolonial performance practices and traditions.

Although every development in performance theory is derived from practice and comes back to guide practice, no distinct theory has emerged in sub-Saharan Africa. This Element is intended to begin the work of addressing this lacuna. Theatre has been practised in Africa since precontact times and includes a variety of forms such as oral panegyric poetry, ritual, festivals, storytelling, choral bards, rites, coronations, partying, celebrations, cultural performance, ceremony, pageants, parades, and military drills. The theatre of creolisation that emerged at the moment of encounter with Semites and western colonials and subsequent formations – such as assimilationist theatre, Negritude theatre, Black Consciousness Theatre, struggle/combat/liberation theatre and national theatre(s) – were 'haunted' by the ghosts of these earlier forms. In addition, the agenda of these later theatre formations was determined by the phase and intensity of struggle against colonial presence, giving African theatre a certain uniqueness not found elsewhere in the world. Contemporary African theatre is 'ghosted' by precontact practices creating a praxis that, as scholars have observed, cannot be understood by the application of western theories which were crafted from a different theatre tradition. Linda Tuhiwai Smith puts it succinctly when she asserts that: 'Indigenous peoples have been, in many ways, oppressed by theory. Any consideration of the way of our origins have been examined, our histories recounted, our arts analysed, our cultures dissected, measured, torn apart and distorted back to us will suggest that theories have not looked sympathetically or ethically at us'(Smith, 2021, p. 42).

Indeed, calls for the decolonisation of theatre have been made since the 1960s and have grown louder in the early twenty-first century not just in Africa but in universities across the globe. My central contention – which provides the rationale for the Element – is that while practitioners have been extremely successful in creating decolonised African theatre, theatre scholars and the academy more broadly have not responded by decolonising their own epistemology. Criticism has continued to be characterised by the application of western theories inadequate to the task of fully appreciating the development of African theatre. In this Element, I set out an African theory of theatre which I call Afroscenology and apply it to and analysis of plays of the African great tradition. My proposed focus is on published plays that have been performed professionally or within university campuses as part of research. These include the works of Wole Soyinka (Nigeria), Dambudzo Marechera (Zimbabwe), Athol Fugard (South Africa), Gcina Mhlophe (South Africa), and Andrew Whaley (Zimbabwe). While these practitioners will partly underpin my discussion, my own positioning in Africa will influence extra choices I make. I was educated in Zimbabwe and South Africa and watched more plays from southern Africa than any other regions of Africa. I am currently working at Wits University in Johannesburg in South Africa. My own creative practice and the works of practitioners in southern Africa will serve as immediate examples to provide evidence to some of my claims.

Afroscenology is a new system of thought that derives its tenets from ancient and contemporary African performance. Afroscenology is a programme of action that guides creativity on the African continent and its diaspora. It could be handy to any creative subject who may find it useful in their context. Afroscenology is an extension of Molefe Asante's Afrocentricity. Afroscenology does not seek to subjugate any other culture and proffer its tenets as the only true ones. It simply offers a different reality while respecting other realities, sometimes even challenging them for their toxic coloniality.

While Afrocentricity has been useful in the field of literature and social analysis, it has not developed any substantial vocabulary to be of significant use in African theatre and serve in addressing ideological issues related to agency, perspective, re-righting history. Afroscenology fills that lacuna by extending its tenets to the field of theatre and performance studies. It provides a system of thought and practice to guide performance, playwrighting, dancing, designing, lighting, and training in such specialised fields. Every theory that extends another theory has a right to stand on its own and establish its own new rules. Postmodernism extends modernism and assumes an identity of its own. Likewise, Afroscenology extends the domains of Afrocentricity in the field of theatre and performance and assumes an identity of its own. Afroscenology stands on the theoretical tenets of Afrocentricity that include reorientation, lexical refinement, centre, agency, and Diopian thought/African subject place.

Afrocentricity is a literary theory which seeks to challenge the intrinsic Eurocentricity of most western theories. Western theory, though useful in some instances, is constructed from a male Eurocentric gaze which is projected as universal and as a result has expunged other ways of knowing. Afrocentricity frames its ideas, concepts, events, personalities, and all processes in the context of Black people occupying subject place and not being objectified (Asante, 2007). Its first tenet is African agency which is connected to subject place. Agency is the capacity to act and the actualisation of this capacity even in circumstances which limit or proscribe such actions. Intentionality in action is part of the expression of agency. Agency in this case is initiated by a Black subject/agent and is distinguished from non-human agency in that it is accompanied by reflection and care about motivation. There are clear desires, beliefs, and intentions exuded by the agent as opposed to irrational behaviour of Black subjects normally projected in western creative works. Agents may control their beliefs through acquisition of epistemes, and it is possible for more than one person to share collective agency and intentionality. Asante (2007) argues that in all experiences where African people feature, we must look for or locate their agency as the tendency in western theory is to invisiblise them or to attack their personhood or to project their actions as irrational, savage, and lacking motive. Asante argues that in all spheres of life of African people, there can be no doubt about African agency and what can be debated is the magnitude of agency and not its absence.

Its second tenet is centre. Centre is an artificial construct created by the coloniser which relies on the peripheralisation of the colonised on the margins. This relationship of centre and the margins continues even after colonisation. The centre becomes the worldview; a centre of values, ethics, episteme, language, and all matters related to human pursuits. What holds for the centre is projected on the margins as the only truth. Afrocentricity creates an alternative centre by 'moving the centre' (wa Thiong'o, 1993) from Europe to Africa. The values, customs, traditions, knowledge, ways, and so on, are then derived from Africa but without forcing them on others as the new Afro-normality. Asante (2007) calls this place an 'intellectual *djed*' which he defines as a stasis or strong place to stand from which critics and creatives should view the world.

Its third tenet is reorientation. This is a programme inherited from the Black Power/Black Consciousness Movements whose focus was to 'cure' Black disorientation created by knowledge systems to support slavery, colonialism, and apartheid. In various parts of the colonial superstructure, western systems were glorified and demeaning Africa and Africans and everything that they possessed or created creating what Asante (2007) calls 'off-centeredness' of Africans. Any critique or knowledge system should reorientate Africans on their truth.

Related to reorientation is what Asante (2007) called Diopian thought. This is a term derived from the African historian, Cheik Diop, who revised western history through scientific methods and proved that the ancient Egyptian civilisation was an African Black civilisation. Africans had a duty in all fields of study to check the accuracy of knowledge especially on Africans and if it was incorrect, it needed to be rewritten and revised. In creative endeavours, these lies and stereotypes they have produced have to be countered through responsible creativity.

Finally, Asante (2007) argued that Africans needed to be committed to lexical refinement to eliminate pejoratives. This entails discarding loaded words and replacing narrow words only capable of espousing western reality while excluding other realities. This is the domain of new theory, concepts, methods, and terminology to describe and frame African phenomena.

Is there a place for Afroscenology after the propounding of Performance theory (Schechner, 1988) or Ethnoscenology (Pradier, 1995)? Afroscenology holds these theories with uttermost respect but is dissatisfied with their lack of place for Africa. All theoretical tenets of the these theories are derived from South America and Asia and (except for Victor Turner, 1988) almost nothing from Africa as if to say there is no practice in Africa. While Performance Studies and Ethnoscenology are liberating, they forget to liberate Africa and are therefore complicit in the unequal power relations. Afroscenology derives its power, strategies, and programme from the creative output of Africans and Africanists in order to offer something new to the world.

When I first publicly proclaimed the theory of Afroscenology at an arts research conference at the University of Cote d'Azur, France, in 2019, I got some very interesting responses, but I want to mention two that stuck with me. The first response was by Professor Gunter Berghaus that he expressed from a place of much anxiety. He acknowledged that western universities needed to be exposed to 'non-western' ways of performance practice and his university had created a position in the drama department to run a course that taught some aspects of what I have called Afroscenology, including running creative outputs. However, he cautioned me against going further with this theory as it would, when fully blown, do exactly what Eurocentric dramatic theories have done. What I took his comment to mean was that it is all right to continue with Afroscenological practice, but to upgrade it to a theory would make it hegemonic. My response to his comment was that Afroscenology should not be confused with Afrocentrism, the opposite of Eurocentrism. In Afrocentrism, the centre moves back to Africa and other cultures would have to give up their values, practices, theories, and episteme in order to embrace the single truth of Afrocentrism. I declared my allegiance to Molefe Asante's Afrocentricity which proposes something uniquely African but offers it to the world without forcing or persuading arts practitioners to give up their centre, values, and knowledge for the African one. It simply says here is our contribution to the world; use it if you find it useful or appropriate it to suit your own context. I then deployed the Steve Biko (2004) argument that African theories should not be feared because they can never be hegemonic. Only those that have power to subjugate others can force and/or persuade the powerless to accept their knowledge as the truth. Even in my wildest imagination, Africa will not wield the power to force its knowledge on others, at least for now and in the foreseeable future.

The second response that stuck with me was from Professor Giaco Schiesser who suggested that the history of colonisation of Africa could not be ignored. A theory that would embrace 'hybridity' because of mixing of cultures would better articulate the creative realities of Africa. He then proclaimed that Afroscenology did not exist. My response was that postcoloniality which celebrates hybridity is only one way of decolonising African theatre, and I have written about that process elsewhere (Ravengai, 2018) but it is certainly not the only legitimate way of disrupting coloniality. I would prefer to use the term 'syncretism' to hybridity as the latter is derived from biology where inherited genes have dominant and recessive formations. If the dominant part is to be always occupied by the former colonial master, African performance identity could not be fully explained by its bastardisation. With syncretism, the creatives decide which framework is to be used as a generative matrix and which texts are to be keyed into the chosen theatrical framework. Indeed, Afroscenology welcomes vitalising contributions from other cultures as long as African performance modes remain dominant.

Long after the conference, a few questions continue to ring in my mind. Most of Asia was colonised by the British and fellow Asian nations like Japan. If this theory of hybridity is mobilised based on colonial contact, then it must apply to all nations with a history of colonisation. I have not seen any scholar raising questions on the right of performance theories from Asia to exist such as Suziki Tadashi's acting method and Indian *Rasa* theory and *Natyasastra* treatise on the arts. Is Africa the only continent that cannot process its practice into theories? Why should it be the only continent whose existence and that of its creative output be understood in relation to its colonisers? Granted, that is unavoidable in some cases, just as in Asia, but surely, some performance forms can still be processed on African terms.

I am proposing that Afroscenology becomes a theoretical lens and a research niche to advance its theoretical tenets and reach where scholars may choose to explore any, but not limited to the following topics:

- Performer training methods advanced by African scholars, practitioners, and activists.
- Ethno-methodologies of researching African theatre practices.
- The ways in which theatre-makers deploy African performance forms on their own or in combination with any transnational influences.
- New curatorial practices in all subfields of theatre (design, acting, writing, dance, voice, directing, etc.) that seek to disrupt colonial epistemology and advance knowledge of how those practices may be disseminated.
- Any politics that may emerge out of which aesthetic/theory to use in assessing new work.
- Development of new vocabularies to explain, describe, and theorise African theatre practices.
- Any conflict that may ensue in training performers, adjudication, assessing new work, and conferring honour on theatre-makers.
- Historiography/Genealogies of African theatre innovations.
- New ways of analysing performance and playtexts that derive their existence from African modes of performance or their combination with transnational influences.
- Application of existing African theories (Womanism, Afrocentricity, Pan-Africanism, postcoloniality/decoloniality, etc.) to playtexts and practices.
- The development of new assessment methods of new playtexts, design, performance, and directing.
- Intersections of materiality and culture, gender studies, race studies, and other areas of human thought and action which seek to challenge relations of power.
- Description, reflection, and documentation of the processes of creating new work and how those processes may suggest a theory of practice.

Afroscenology is not a disinterested theory. It is developing out of a history of colonisation and inequality. Most drama/theatre/performance departments, for example, in South Africa were established during colonial/apartheid era. They were modelled on the British or American frameworks. At independence/

freedom, the departments continued business as usual. The postcolonial academy is oftentimes the last bastion of coloniality. It took student and staff demonstrations in Kenya, Zimbabwe, and South Africa for the authorities to foreground decolonisation in their planning programmes. The theories used to study material, even the ones developed in Africa, came from the West. Examples and case studies were (and in some universities still) largely from the West. The epistemes and creative outputs are therefore not geared towards delivering the kinds of knowledge and understanding that are adequate to addressing long-standing issues of coloniality and the attendant issue of unequal power. The psychophysical method developed by Constantin Stanislavsky and the many permutations of his method have created a global system that threatens to decimate epistemological difference. Afroscenology is against globalism and universality and advocates for difference and relativism on all matters secular. As Steve Biko (2004) has clearly indicated, to strive to learn something from another culture which comes naturally to the owners of that culture is to agree that one will never be as good as its owner. This scenario creates an unequal relationship where the African subject will forever be a learner while his white counterpart assumes the role of a teacher. Frantz Fanon echoes the same sentiments when he writes:

> So comrades, let us not pay tribute to Europe by creating states, institutions and societies that draw inspiration from it. Humanity expects other things from us than this grotesque and generally obscene emulation. If we want to transform Africa into a new Europe, then let us entrust the destinies of our countries to the Europeans. They will do a better job than the best of us. But, if we want humanity to take one step forward, if we want to take it to another level than the one where Europe has placed it, then we must innovate, we must be pioneers. (1963b, p. 239)

To date, mainstream performer training in African universities is dominated by the 'method' system that has alienated many African students, especially those brought up in the African townships and rural areas who embody a different playing culture (see Ravengai, 2011). Coloniality inherent in some African universities has made sure that these African students give up this playing culture/embodiment as soon as they enter the academy. The goal of Afroscenology is radical transformation. Afroscenology challenges the sustenance of existing power structures by dismantling the system to reform it.

Afroscenology theory is characterised by three basic structures, two of which are subsumed in the term, narratology. The third structure is the performatic theory/technique. Narratology is used here to mean an engagement with or study of stories/narratives, the way they are organised in some kind of structure and how this organisation of structural components influences the perceiver/

analyst's reception. After studying several plays now forming the African great tradition/canon, one notices recurring features in these narratives that give them an identity very much different from the dramatic narrative theorised by Aristotle as dramatic theory. I have called the first part of African narratology the 'theatric theory' to distinguish it from the Aristotelian dramatic theory. While dramatic theory is best illustrated by a Freytag pyramid structure, the theatric theory is characterised by a series of semicircular compressions with several cantos within them to be explained below hereafter. Each compression ends with a discontinuity, or dislocation, or quasi-stasis. The final compression will have a similar structure but ends with a deformation. In a nutshell, the African story written through the lens of Afroscenology has an 'exposition' which introduces the problem/issue/subject or the inciting incident and the characters. This could happen using song, music, dance, a narrator, or chorus/ bards, or duologue, or a creative combination of any of these elements. The basic tenets of the theatric theory discussed at length in Section 3 are as follows:

- Exposition
- Compression
- Canto
- Discontinuity
- Deformation

The second structure subsumed under African narratology is an aspect which may be called focalisation, translated as *Zivo*, *Tsebo*, and *Ulwazi* in Shona, Sotho, and Zulu respectively, meaning 'knowledge' or what Keir Elam (1993) calls epistemic, ideological, and psychological codes. All plays have a story which conveys a philosophy or advances an episteme conveyed from a specific point of view/perspective. Afroscenology derives these special codes from what, in the past, was called Black Aesthetics or revolutionary aesthetics (see Taylor, 2016, Chifunyise and Kavanagh, 1988; Udenta, 1993). The most important aspects covered under these codes are:

- An African perspective.
- Visiblising and protecting the Black personhood.
- Privileging Black political thought whatever form it may take.
- Commitment to African spirituality.
- Commitment to the pursuit of African autonomy.
- Construction of African characters that are types and giving them subject place.
- Construction of positive heroes from the subaltern characters: villagers, peasants, working class, lumpen proletariat, women, and children.
- Democratisation of language.

- Deploying of Afrocentricity as a creative method and pursuing its tenets: agency, subject place, centre/Afriway, Diopian thought, reorientation, and lexical refinement as explained previously.

The third and last structure of Afroscenology is what I have called the 'performatic theory'. This is the theory of performer training that derives its praxis from the African canon. It is a developing theory and it is currently anchored by nine tenets. Section 4 explains a few of these tenets with a major focus on Afrosonic mime.

- Hyper-imagination/imagistic imagination
- Afrosonic mime
- Vectorisation
- Organicity
- Physical action
- Bifurcation
- Etudes
- Spirituality
- Kinetic tableaux

Several works on decolonisation of literature in general and theatre in particular have emerged since the 1960s. All of them agree on one fundamental issue that western epistemology has emasculated Africa's ability to think for itself. They have been successful in developing the language of critique to engage Eurocentrism. A few examples can be cited to support this claim. Ali Mazrui (2009), for example, devoted his scholarship to critiquing Eurocentrism and coined some interesting concepts to engage with its biases such as Euro-heroism, Euro-mitigation, Euro-exclusivity, denying credit to the achievement of others, apportioning disproportionate blame to the sins of others, short-changing other cultures, and looking at other cultures from a western perspective. When Eurocentrism achieves the aforementioned, it creates a kind of common sense where everything non-western has to be seen as a deviation from the norm. This is what Kaviraj called 'Euro-normality' (2009, p. 189). Ngugi wa Thiong'o advanced the work begun by the Black Power and Black Consciousness Movements by not engaging the West and its injustices but by addressing African people to decolonise their minds by means of imbibing African epistemology and deploying African languages in creative writing. In his *Decolonising the Mind* (1987), wa Thiong'o focuses on writing African literature (including dramatic literature) in African languages as he sees language as the carrier of culture and reservoir of knowledge. In his *Moving the Centre* (1993), he focused on centring African literatures in the comparative literature curriculum and then radiate outwards by studying other literatures but from an African centre.

The issue of language was to inspire a huge debate in African decolonisation which spilled into the 1990s.

Some African writer-scholars like Chinua Achebe (1975) and Wole Soyinka (1976) and literary scholars like Chidi Amuta (1989) and Chinweizu et al. (1980) believed that decolonisation could take place within English language by domesticating it and making it African through several linguistic strategies such as productive hybridisation, interlingualism, translanguaging, relexification, pidginisation, and direct translation. Others like wa Thiong'o (1987) believed that decolonisation of literature would be more radical if Africans exercised their creativity in major African languages. The debate was quite sustained and to follow the merits and demerits of each of these positions would drift us from the main agenda of contextualising the niche of this Element, which is decolonisation of theory.

Herbert Isaac Ernest Dhlomo was arguably the first African to attempt to theorise his practice and that of his tribespeople. He lived between the period 1903 and 1956 in South Africa, writing dozens of plays, very few of which exist today (see Couzens, 1985). He theorised what he practised by contributing essays to a journal called *Bantu Studies* (1939) and other magazines. He theorised his practice under the conceptual term, *izibongelo*, which he defined as covering 'all forms of tribal dramatic art' (Dhlomo, 1939, p. 48). Like Sam Ukala, discussed hereafter, who examined African storytelling and came up with eight laws, Dhlomo looked at Nguni praise poetry (*izibongo*), *ingoma* dances, and festivals and observed key tenets which he suggested should be grafted in African playtexts. He demonstrated his theory by writing several plays which evidenced some of these tenets. It must be noted that the dominant African theory amongst African intellectuals of his time was Negritudism. Negritude playwrights sought to rehabilitate the degraded African personhood by writing stories which glorified their achievements. He wrote plays about historical kings of the Sotho, *Moshoeshoe,* and Zulu, *Dingane* and *Cetshwayo* (Dhlomo et al., 1985). While the content was African including some African performance modes, this content was subsumed in the Aristotelian dramatic structure/form. As I have argued elsewhere, Ravengai (2018), when African performance modes are keyed into the western dramaturgical frame, both structure and African performance modes are altered to form something new. To advance this practice, Dhlomo theorised on 'syncretism' by suggesting that:

> The development of African drama cannot be purely from African roots. It must be grafted in western drama. It must borrow from, be inspired by, shoot from European dramatic art forms, and tainted by exotic influences. The African dramatist must not fear being mocked as an 'imitator' of European art. (1977, p. 7)

However, Dhlomo qualified this assertion. The playwright should not be entirely Eurocentric. The work must reflect their 'soul' and 'individuality'. In fact, Dhlomo emphasised not so much 'what is done' but 'how it is done' which speaks to form. This is an aspect he explained in other tenets of his theory.

Though Dhlomo never used the term I suggest here, I would call his second tenet, *'performativeness'*, which I use to mean that which makes theatrical performance different from ordinary everyday performance. Erving Goffman (1974) uses the term everyday performance to cover ad hoc performances which normally occur in domestic settings, for example, bending knees during greetings, showing appreciation by clapping hands, playing a musical instrument randomly, work performances such as construction, rescue operations, and so on. Here, there is no careful curating of performance elements through the agency of a director or playwright to cause *performativeness* to occur. Dhlomo, in fact, used the words action, rhythm, emotion, gesture, imitation, and desires (1977, p. 3) to describe what I call *performativeness*. Dhlomo argued that traditional African theatre did not pursue what formalists called a 'fabula' or in Shona, *rondedzero* (to mean a story or an account of something) or what Dhlomo called propaganda or didacticism, but it pursued pleasure through the spectacle of action carried in dance, gesture, rhythm, costumes, and make up. The 'how it is done' would be equivalent to what the formalist called *'syuzhet'* which is a Russian term to describe how meaning bearing texts like song, dance, poetry, and narrative are arranged for beauty. The Shona call this phenomenon, *kurongeka*, meaning the way things are organised to create order. This *syuzhet* or *kurongeka* is a source of satisfying beauty which contributes to variation and the conveying of abstract and even concrete ideas of the performance. This *performativeness* captures the attention of the audience giving them satisfying pleasure similarly offered in literature by the literariness of language. The Shona call this satisfying beauty and pleasure which result from an orderly arrangement of objects, things, and issues, *kushongedzeka*. The arrangement of these elements in an African play is covered in Figure 2. *Performativeness* which inheres in all African plays helps to create an atmosphere, an orientation, a feeling, or emotions not reducible to a fabula/ *rondezero*. The fabula may be contained in a canto but the next one may not have a causal relationship with the last one. It is this quality of an African performance which Dhlomo wanted grafted into the modern African play.

> Today, in music, in poetry, in dancing, in drama, painting and architecture, men seek new forms, idioms and styles of technique to express the ever-green artistic impulse. Cannot Africa infuse new blood into the weary limbs of the older dramatic forms of Europe? Are African scholars and artists and writers incapable of creating something fresh and young from these archaic tribal artistic forms? (1939, p. 48)

These are very important questions which this Element tries to answer by propounding the theory of Afroscenology. Dhlomo theorised on the tenet of joint performance where there is no line of demarcation between the audience and performers. This is an aspect also recognised in postdramatic theatre under the rubric, metaxis. His last declared tenet was spirituality which he argued was part of African reality as it aided performers in realising character, in dancing, singing, and reciting poetry (*izibongo*). He foregrounded what he called modern theories which support the idea that, in using spirituality, the African was not merely superstitious. Behind this practice lay a source of esoteric knowledge which was useful for the African to be spontaneous in performance and to be prolific in speech.

Towards the beginning of the 1990s, the critiquing of western epistemology was moving towards more solid suggestions on how this knowledge was to be countered and contained. In concluding his debate on language, Chidi Amuta (1989) devoted an entire chapter to African theatre where he asserted the importance of a playwright's commitment to the struggles of Africa. If African playwrighting was to be revolutionary in the cause of African people, the thematic revolution was to be carried through 'revolutionary dramatic techniques' (1989, p. 156). He advocated for a reformulation of 'an anti-imperialist aesthetics' which depended on the rich heritage of African playing culture to articulate modern issues. He did not write what the aesthetic could possibly look like. Towards the end of his book, *Decolonising the Mind*, Ngugi wa Thiong'o (1987) devoted a chapter to what he called 'The Language of African Theatre' and he was closer to adumbrating a theory of African theatre than he thought. He mentioned dance, song, mime, and text as some of the characteristics of this African aesthetic.

By the mid-1990s, more concrete descriptions of the African theory were emerging. I would call these descriptions, antecedents to the theory of Afroscenology which this Element engages with. In 1996, Sam Ukala named the African theatre aesthetic, 'folkism' (Ukala, 1996). He began his argument by getting entangled in the language debate in the context of Nigerian theatre and suggested an engineered English domesticated to carry the weight and depth of Nigerian culture. He then explained folkism as the use of history, culture, concerns, and aspirations of Nigerian people to compose and perform deploying African conventions. The folktale or ritual would be used as the generative matrix into which other texts would be grafted to produce something unique. By 2001, Ukala had fully developed this theoretical proposal which now extended to the rest of the continent. He may have seen that the individual national theatre aesthetics espoused by various African countries were converging on similar issues of using storytelling or ritual to create new works. He called the theory

'African alternative theatre aesthetic'. Given that the aesthetic was an alternative to the dominant western one at the time, it was important to modify it with the term 'alternative' which would be a misnomer in the current setup where the technique is becoming dominant in Africa. He crafted eight laws of the theory which he named the law of opening, the law of joint performance, the law of creativity, free enactment and responsibility, law of audience evaluation, law of audience questioning, the law of audience's free expression of emotions, the law of audience interjections, and the law of closing (Ukala, 2001, pp. 38–39). This theory was derived from African storytelling and would preclude differently crafted plays. However, the proposal was brave. Section 2 will briefly look into this history of African artist-researchers who grappled with the idea of an African aesthetic.

An important Africanist who contributed to the theorisation of African theatre is Robert Mshengu Kavanagh (alias Robert Malcolm McLaren). After starting an experimental theatre company, Workshop '71 in South Africa with African collaborators and editing several issues of *Sketch* – a magazine dedicated to Black South African theatre, he pursued doctoral studies in theatre at Leeds University. His thesis was converted into a book, *Theatre and Cultural Struggle in South Africa* (1985), dedicated to the study of African theatre in South Africa, applying radical Marxist theory. He then settled in Zimbabwe where he experimented with African modes of performance in his theatre company, Zambuko/Izibuko, and with University of Zimbabwe students where he was a senior lecturer. Together with Stephen Chifunyise and Ngugi wa Mirii, they developed a type of African theatre which they variously called 'democratic theatre', 'revolutionary theatre', 'national theatre', and later 'people's theatre'. While the descriptors kept shifting, the techniques deployed were the same. This African technique is exhaustively explained in his book, *Making People's Theatre* (1997a) which was later reprinted as *Making Theatre* (2016b). Kavanagh's latest article uses the descriptor 'African non-realist theatre' (2022) to describe the same practice. Read together, these works propose a theory which he connects to my term, Afroscenology, especially in his latest article on African non-realism. He proposes a theory of making theatre characterised by improvisation/etudes, exploration, open rehearsals, organic casting, democratic directing, heightened performance, mime, dance, and performing songs. He uses the term eclectic theatre to describe a situation where African theatre is composed from a variety of African performance modes, a condition sometimes referred to as parataxis, borrowing from linguistics where words, phrases, clauses, or sentences are set next to each other so that each element is equally important. In the case of theatre, songs, dances, music, mime, and poetry are brought to bear on the playtext without each of these becoming more dominant than others. In the holistic sense, the theatre communicates through symbolism rather than didacticism. On this issue, Dhlomo and Kavanagh intersect.

Kavanagh converges with Udenta Udenta (1993) on the use of the terms 'democratic drama/theatre' and 'revolutionary theatre/aesthetics'. Both created and wrote from a Marxist perspective. While Kavanagh wrote his African non-realist theory from the perspective of performance and production, Udenta wrote about the same theory from a literary perspective covering what Pieter Fourie (1988) calls narrative and thematic codes or for the same concepts what Keir Elam (1993) calls epistemic and ideological codes. Udenta was responding to a branch of critical realism espoused by African liberal humanists who used satire to critique everything about the new independent African states, their leadership, and society but without engaging with systemic issues caused by capitalist structures left intact by colonialism. This literature and theatre were advanced by petty-bourgeois writers who benefitted from colonial education or theatre groups sponsored by foreign embassies and so-called Non-Governmental Organisations to create what Udenta calls 'the drama of neo-colonial dependency' (1993, p. 26) or what Chifunyise and Kavanagh call 'the neocolonial road' (1988, p. 2). Udenta then propounded the epistemic/narrative tenets of revolutionary theatre. These included the issue of perspective and worldview of the subaltern, observation of the laws of dialectics where the story depicted the different phases of social development and the victory of subalterns, typification of characters, construction and depiction of positive heroes from the subalterns, deployment of socialist realism as a creative method, democratisation of language by making it relevant and accessible to all people and on a performative level, and allowance of joint performance with the audience.

The twenty-first century saw a renewed vigour by African scholars to name and describe the aesthetic. Kennedy Chinyowa propounded what he called 'an aesthetic theory for African popular theatre'. Writing from an applied theatre perspective, he prescribed what he called 'play' as the spine of his theory which he argued was the structuring element in the process of communicating development. Such 'play' inhered in storytelling, ritual, music, song, dance, poetry, drumming, and masquerade (Chinyowa, 2007, 2015). At closer examination, what Ngugi wa Thiong'o called 'the language of African theatre' is what Chinyowa called 'play'. Chinyowa went further to describe this 'play' and offered make-believe, liminality, imitation, improvisation, and domestication of such practices, as its various tenets.

Awo Asiedu (2011) discussed developments on decolonisation of theatre through retheorisation. She stressed the need to theorise African experiences.

She used the terms, '*Anansegoro*' and '*Abibigoro*', concepts used by Akan theatre practitioners to refer to Black theatre using a storytelling matrix. This technique would deploy one or more storytellers, a group of musicians correctly named 'players' to provide musical interludes, dancers, and mime performers, allowing for audience participation as captured in Ukala's theoretical tenets. Although the *anansegoro* and *abibigoro* techniques could be used to craft a theory of African theatre, Asiedu ended by making a plea for retheorisation of African theatre: 'There is need for modern-day African Aristotle who will rise to the occasion to capture and describe current theatre practices across the continent which would in the future serve as an African poetics for the study of African theatre.'(2011, p. 380)

I hope that this Element partly answers to that call by looking at the structure of African theatrical texts in Section 3 and describing one of the tenets of the African performatic technique, Afrosonic mime, and how it works in African performance in Section 4.

Towards the beginning of the 2020s, two philosophical works emerged dealing with the singularity of blackness and the ensuing creative works which furthered the philosophy/discourse of Black people. It was Achille Mbembe's *Critique of Black Reason* (2017) and Charles Taylor's *Black Is Beautiful: A Philosophy of Black Aesthetics* (2016). What these two books successfully argued for was that one side of Black reason/discourse was dominated by western conjectures which condemned blackness as a single sign. The second side of Black reason/discourse responded to the condemnation also as a single voice to defend the denuded Black sign, filling the emptiness with something of value. As the politics that people were dealing with were different at different times (slavery, invasion, colonisation, assimilation, radical decolonisation, neocolonialism, etc.), responses to these evils of their time also took different forms, but similar during each period. Taylor noticed these cultural formations during these various phases of Black torment: premodernity, creolisation, civilisationism, counter-modernity, radical decolonisation, and postblackness (Taylor, 2016, pp. 13–19). These creative formations took specific stylistic forms which can be described and theorised. After the persuasive arguments of these scholars on African responses to western conjectures, I feel that it is no longer necessary to write a long justification on the provenance and occurrence of an African aesthetic. This Element will go straight into describing and theorising the aesthetic under the conceptual term, Afroscenology.

In the colonial/apartheid/slavery past, scholars referred to the theatre created by Black people to respond to western conjectures, Black theatre. The aesthetic which emerged from the practice of Black theatre was called Black Aesthetics. To be concise, no one except Black theatre practitioners could practice Black theatre. However, the philosophers of Black theatre did not wish that this theatre be an end in itself. It was a means to an end, that is, fighting and ending white oppression. In the words of the coiner of 'Black Theatre', Steve Biko, 'the Black Consciousness approach would be irrelevant in a colourless and non-exploitative egalitarian society' (2004, p. 96). This is a point echoed by another Black Theatre philosopher, Mafika Gwala (1973), where he argued that Black Theatre is 'a temporary thing' while the search for national theatre ensues. By national theatre, Gwala meant a type of theatre which embraced features of performance from all people living in South Africa but without assimilating into western culture. It could embrace western tenets but these would be deployed on the terms dictated by African performance. In other words, the generative matrix would be African. He argued that the term 'Black theatre' must fall into disuse when social conditions which shaped it disappeared. Clearly, colonialism and apartheid have ended, although the structures which they created continue to have a life in contemporary African society. What I am proposing in this Element is not a Black aesthetic to be exclusively deployed by Black theatre-makers. That would demean Africa's contribution to the world economy of performance if only one race were to apply the theory. While some of its characteristics bear the DNA of Black aesthetics, what is subsumed in Afroscenology is an African practice developed by both Africans and Africanists (non-Africans) interested in the advancement of African practices. It is in this context that I use the concept, Afroscenology, to name the new theory.

While different scholars adumbrated on creating a national theatre and invariably a national aesthetic, it became clear that what was being proposed in different geopolitical settings bore the same characteristics which I have given the global name, Afroscenology. Scholars with a literary background like Chidi Amuta (1989), Chinweizu et al. (1980), and Charles Taylor (2016) have covered sufficient ground on what Keir Elam (1980) calls cultural, epistemic, and ideological codes of the African theatrical text. These are theatrical codes which provide a system of rules for producing and interpreting signs shared by communities of meaning. While applying Marxist and Afrocentric theories, they came to some conclusion that the playwright/theatre maker had to have commitment and responsibilities to the cause of Africa and Africans. They had the responsibility to make the work 'relevant' and intelligible. If syncretism was part of creativity, it was supposed to be pursued within the parameters of African tradition where it was the major feature of the creative work. Such creativity was for purposes of modernising and/or revitalising folk art to promote preservation and change. In terms of commitment, the playwright needed to refine the work's quality and be intentional about its political orienta-tion and the perceptions it engendered. These had to advance the cause of Africans. From a literary perspective, Chinweizu et al. gave guidelines to the

African critic on the criteria they needed to use to engage with the work. One cannot change the aesthetic and fail to change the assessment scheme. Charles Taylor, relying on Molefe's theory of Afrocentricity singled out a couple of epistemic and ideological codes which were to inhere in the African aesthetic, visiblising Black characters and giving them agency, protecting the Black personhood from misrepresentation, discarding stereotypes, fostering Black perspectives on issues, and advancing Black politics, whatever form it may take. In terms of political codes, it is important to capture Taylor's exact words: '(i) The explicit adoption of black point of view; (ii) commitment to communalism; (iii) commitment to spirituality; (iv) insistence on an organic link between theory and practice and (v) a commitment to the pursuit of black autonomy, whether for individuals, institutions, or the race as a whole.'(2016, p. 81)

While the ideological and epistemic codes are quite clear and need no emphasis, this Element focuses on the whole theatrical code as a system with its subcodes of form. Sections 2–4 contribute to this debate by adding the history of artistic research and the findings which ensued to develop Afroscenology. Section 3 contextualises types of African theatrical texts and delineates structural elements. I select one type of African texts which I call *rombic* theatre. Western theories and philosophies condemn this type of theatre as poor or aberrant imitations of western absurd theatre. I recall producing Dambudzo Marechera's *The Alley* at the Wits Theatre in 2017 and my white colleagues who came to watch it did not see it as fully absurd and indeed, they were correct. One can say the same about Wole Soyinka's play of the *rombe* type. Section 3 gives the roots of African *rombic* theatre (not to be confused with western absurd theatre) and then craft a theory based on the examples of plays following this schema. I write this alternative theory from a sense of deep anxiety emanating from what Nigam calls 'an immense dissatisfaction with the way dominant hegemonic theory pronounces its judgement on the rest of the world' (2020, p. 48). I call this theory of the playtext, the theatric theory. The performatic technique is a book-length discussion but I have elected one of its tenets, Afrosonic mime, to explain it in Section 4. Clearly, this Element is an introduction to the theory of Afroscenology and a follow-up monograph will be required to exhaust all its tenets. Section 5 concludes this element summarising the findings and suggesting ways in which this theory can be expanded.

2 Reconfiguring African Theatre Episteme: Formulating the Theory of Afroscenology

Since all practices either follow an existing theory or propose a new one, artistic research has the potential to propose and advance new theories. In this section,

I argue that arts researchers in African theatre have been developing new techniques and processes since 1939, based on African performance modes and their creative recombination with multinational influences to create work that is unique to the African continent. I have called this creative theory 'Afroscenology'. I see artistic research as offering the opportunity to create knowledge based on African practice and produced from our local context. This section will delineate these seven approaches to artistic research. Since the other six approaches are relatively well known, I will spend a little more time explicating how artistic research can lead to the invention of a new theory, in this case, Afroscenology.

The Context of Artistic Research

The fight for recognition of artistic practice as research began in the 1980s when the South African Department of Education (as it was then called) introduced a new funding regime where public universities would receive state subsidy based on the quantum of traditional research, as well as doctoral and master's graduates. The state did not recognise creative output as research. At least in South Africa, where the number of theatre departments and staff is higher than that of Zimbabwe, these departments used their numerical advantage to influence policy on artistic research. By the late 1990s, some South African universities established internal recognition systems for creative outputs and allowed artistic researchers to advance their careers based on recognition of their creative outputs as research. Around the same time, artistic research had become a well-established approach as a method of enquiry in the UK, Australia, Canada, and Scandinavia.

In Zimbabwe, without any pressure from artistic researchers, the few universities (Midlands State University, University of Zimbabwe, and Great Zimbabwe University) offering drama/theatre/performance created staffing and promotion ordinances that recognised creative output as research. They would reward artistic researchers if their creative output displayed 'originality and innovation in contribution to issues of culture, of creative arts, writing, architectural design, etc.' (MSU Ordinance 5 2010). Regrettably, no one has ever been promoted based on artistic research as the staffing and promotions committees are dominated by academics who are not artistic researchers and are biased towards *scripto-centrism*. The advocacy prevalent in South Africa may, one day, shift attitudes towards artistic research in Zimbabwe.

Despite the strong artistic research advocacy present in South Africa, the government did not change the policy on research until 2017. Not all policies on what constituted research included artistic research as a form of knowing.

The National Plan for Higher Education (NPHE) was, however, warming up to the idea of artistic research by 2001 when it acknowledged the fragility of all preceding policies on research, which were biased against certain disciplines in the arts and humanities. The South African Department of Higher Education and Training (DoHET) finally incorporated recommendations of the NPHE and various documents developed by academics at various forums about artistic research. DoHET developed a new document called *Policy on the Evaluation of Creative Outputs and Innovations* produced by South African Public Higher Education Institutions (2017). This document created six subfields from which artistic research would be assessed and rewarded: fine arts and visual arts, music, theatre/performance/dance, design, film and television, and literary arts. It also provided criteria for assessing artistic research output and the processes that artist-researchers would follow in submitting that research for government subsidy.

After establishing this context, it is necessary to describe the various approaches to how academics carry out artistic research in Africa and motivations for such ways of doing research. My experience in artistic research has taught me that it may take any of the following dimensions.

Artistic research may involve the accumulation of data that confirms an existing theory. This is the place of workshop theatre, variously called devised theatre, collaborative theatre, or radical theatre. The artist-researcher may work from an existing archive, such as the Magnet Theatre's history plays, which rely on memory sites in Cape Town, such as District Six Museum, graveyards, or the Bleek-Lloyd archive, containing Khoisan stories. Magnet Theatre selects the material and subjects it to various playmaking processes with the result of a theatrical output. Workshop theatre may depend on the living archive: people who were actually present during the unfolding of a unique historical moment, for example, the liberation war of Zimbabwe. Based on individual experiences, the artist-researcher selects the material. Zambuko Theatre created frontline theatre based on the experiences of war collaborators (those who were collaborating with guerrilla armies against Rhodesian Forces) who had become students shortly after the war. Zimbabwe Foundation for Education with Production (ZIMFEP) war plays such as *Takaitora neRopa* (Won by Blood) were created by demobilised soldiers under the directorship of artist-researchers, Ngũgĩ wa Mĩriĩ and Kimani Gecau. It is possible that the artist-researcher will follow a pre-existing performance theory in realising the performance. It may also be possible that the artist-researcher will propose a new performance/emplotment/acting theory. It is not an 'either/or' situation. Both old and new theories may inhabit the same performance.

Related to the aforementioned approach is the application of an existing theory to facts, plays, performances, and so on. In this approach, the work already exists in written form as a musical score, a play, dance notation, a literary work, and so on. The artist-researcher chooses, again, an already existing theory to apply to the work. This type of artistic research has always been the norm in the western-influenced academy. An artist-researcher would choose a realist play and deploy realism in transforming the play into a performance. The designers would be guided by the same theory in the construction of sets, costumes, musical, and lighting scores. An acting method designed for realism – the psycho-technique, or its western variations – would be used to guide the performers in researching and constructing characters. Of late, a new generation of artist-researchers has emerged, who seek the death of the playwright, replacing them with the auteur director. This artist-researcher deploys postmodernism as a method of emplotment, where they build a performance text from several sources. The resultant creative output privileges the body over text, exuding a visual dramaturgy. Mncedisi Shabangu, Mandla Mbothwe, Mark Fleishman, and Prince Lamla are South African examples that come to mind.

Artistic research may involve the generation of new theory and its empirical testing. The nexus between performance practice and performance theory, especially in Africa, necessitates that every innovative practical approach in performance preparation, presentation, and training leads to a theory of performance. African performance practices are thoroughly under-theorised. Some South African theatre-makers, for example, have been creating work that is peculiar to their location: making it different from global trends. The 1980s up to the present moment produced work that was uniquely South African with a particular identity of its own as opposed to doing theatre originating from elsewhere in South Africa. A number of these performance forms were appropriated by postliberation theatre-makers to create work and a form of performance practice uniquely South African. Yet the theory of this theatre-making is barely visible. I have in mind the performance practices of Gibson Kente, Mbongeni Ngema, Percy Mtwa, Barney Simon, Mark Fleishman (Magnet Theatre), and Mncedisi Shabangu, in South Africa, to mention but a few. The performance practices developed by these practitioners have revolutionised and expanded our understanding of acting and actor training. The global theory of the actor can, thus, no longer fully explain the developments in Southern African performance. In actor training, there is an overreliance on global notions of acting based on prominent western/eastern theatre innovators and theorists like Konstantin Stanislavski, Anton Chekhov, and Stanford Meisner. Today, we find out that decolonial discourses are frustrated with the lack of African knowledges of performer training. I shall return to this point shortly.

The generation of new methods for dealing with problems in the discipline or in practice – artistic research – has helped us to create a method of research called Practice as Research (PaR). This method is defined as 'research that is carried out through or by means of performance, using methodologies and specific methods familiar to performance practitioners, and where the output is at least in part, if not entirely, presented through performance' (Fleishman, 2012, p. 28).

Temple Hauptfleisch has added three more approaches to artistic research, which I wish to summarise here. He calls the first artistic research approach 'a study *of* the arts' (Hauptfleisch, 2005, p. 19). This is the orthodox tradition where the play/production and its associated assemblage like design, performance, lighting, sound, dance, etc. are taken as the object of study to produce journal articles, collections, monographs, and conference papers. The second approach is one that Hauptfleisch calls arts research as 'a study undertaken *through/by means of* the arts' (2005, p. 19). Here, the process of creative writing, painting, choreography, directing, designing, filmmaking, digital coding, curating, for example, is seen as research. The artist is making discoveries (philosophical thought) as they create and make them known to the audience/analyst. The creative output is the research. The third approach, according to Hauptfleisch, is 'arts research as the development of *new technologies and instruments* for use by artists' (2005, p. 20). This is related to the approach of developing new theories, techniques, and processes that I mentioned, except that, here, a tangible scientific product is the outcome. This may be a new light, new paint, new instrument, for example, of a musical nature. A colleague, Jonathan Crossley (2017), in the Music Department at Wits University manufactured a new guitar, for instance, and that became part of their doctoral thesis. The invention is usually then patented.

Framing the Research

Not all creative activity and practice, even of the highest quality, constitute research. However, creative activity can be distinguished from creative research even if the output resembles each other. Creative activity becomes research when it has been framed as research. Therefore, a framing document should be constructed. The reviewer uses the framing document to evaluate the creative work. In other words, the artist-researcher is helping the reviewer to read their work according to their own criteria. Examples of the questions that reviewers may pose while reading/watching your work may include:

- How does the theatre piece/process relate to the framing?
- Does the theatre piece contribute to current practice or propose something novel? If so, how and to what extent?
- What is the theatre-maker's personal signature/contribution relative to the context? Quality is not the only criterion, but one of the indices of evaluation.

Jon Whitmore has introduced an interesting concept of framing systems (Whitmore, 1994). He argues that audience members or theatre analysts bring the totality of their experiences to watch theatre and may experience it according to their horizon of expectation. To guide the analyst, the artist-researcher should put framing systems in place, and he suggests some of the following:

- Aesthetic framing: This involves a production concept and how it inspired other creative processes.
- Production framing: This involves an element of intellectual involvement, which may take the form of literary/performance analysis, something normally covered in a press release.
- Physical framing: This includes digital drawings of the set, models, sketches, costume, pictures, and so on.
- Intellectual, historical, and social framing: This can be fulfilled by providing a statement of intent outlining the problem or question to be addressed; the researcher contextualises the enquiry. What place does the creative practice occupy in the stylistics, politics, the body of theory, and the researcher's own previous work? Awareness of other theatre-makers' work in the same domain is critical. Positioning the researcher's previous work (where it exists), reputation, and performance style is recommended. State the niche that the new work occupies in the scheme of things.

Towards the Theory of Afroscenology

I now return to artistic research that leads to the generation of a new theory. This nexus between performance practice and performance theory in Africa and the diaspora needs to be theorised. Every innovative practical approach in performance preparation, presentation, and training leads to a theory of performance. While, in the past, alternative modes of theatre analysis, theatre-making/writing, performer training, and performance were not recognised by the dominant western knowledge system, Richard Schechner began theorising Performance Studies in his important book, *Performance Theory*. In 1995, French scholar, Jean-Marie Pradier, coined the term 'ethnoscenology' to describe modes of performance originating from outside North America and Europe or the West (Pradier, 1995). This theory or field of study opens the generation of new terminology to describe and analyse performances that originate from other continents, where western models would not suffice as tools of analysis or creativity. While I recognise the good intentions of Pradier and his theory of ethnoscenology, scholars who have deployed this theory, such as Patrice Pavis (2003) and including those who have deployed Schechner's performance theory, have taken these theories to mean the study of Latin American and Asian performances. As with many other books written from a western perspective, Africa is missing from the map, despite its various performances that have taken place since time immemorial. The underlying assumption is that there is nothing worthy of studying from Africa. A source of irritation is reading any book on performance studies/theatre studies; case studies from Africa are missing. Take, for instance, Meyer-Dinkgräfe's *Approaches to Acting: Past and Present* (2001). It delves into the origins of acting and its evolution in the West from Greece and Rome through the Middle Ages and renaissance periods. Acting developed from declamatory to *commedia dell'arte*, melodramatic acting, and realistic/psychological acting styles. Meyer-Dinkgräfe delineates the challenges to realism by means of expressionist modes of acting, leading to immediacy and presence associated with postdramatic theatre. From the middle of the book, Meyer-Dinkgräfe diverts to what he calls non-western (itself a problematic term) approaches to acting. The case studies cover India, Japan, China, and Islamic countries, and then forges a technique he calls intercultural theatre based on the works of western directors like Peter Brook, who went to the East to harvest stories and techniques to create work such as *The Mahabharata* (2001). Africa is missing.

It has become necessary that researchers from the African continent, or whoever is interested in the study of African performances, do something to fill this lacuna. African theatre-makers like Ngũgĩ wa Thiong'o, Credo Mutwa, Herbert Dhlomo, Gibson Kente, Mbongeni Ngema, Fatima Dike, Percy Mtwa and, of late, younger practitioners like Mandla Mbotwe and Mncedisi Shabangu have been creating work and writing or talking about it. When we look back in relation to the present, we find out characteristics of this work that point to a common artistic practice. Since most, if not all, theory comes from practice, I am advancing the theory of Afroscenology to explain, describe, make, and analyse work that has emerged in Africa. Since this is a neologism, I need to spend a little bit more time explaining the theory before I refer to specific case studies.

The term Afroscenology is formed from three lexical items; 'Afro-', 'scene', and '-logy'. The first lexical item is the root word for Africa from which several words can be formed, such as Africanity, Afrocentricity, Africanism, Afro-hair, or Afro-currency. 'Afro-' denotes a deep interest in Africa and a rootedness in the continent and its epistemes. 'Scene' has Greco-Roman origins. The Greek word is '*skene*', which means tent or stage, and the Latin version is '*scena*' meaning the same thing. The English version, 'scene', has several meanings that, in play, denotes an action that happens at the same place and time. Outside art, it means a place, activity, or in crime, a place where an unpleasant event happened. From this word, various English words are formed, such as scenery, scenario, and scenic. All these words project objects that can be seen whether as art or in their natural environments, or a sequence of events that build a narrative of a specific nature. Thus, in western culture, the art of building sets and costumes for performances is called scenography. The lexical item '-logy' does not exist on its own. It is a suffix normally used in English to form new terminologies that refer to a field of study, a branch of knowledge, bodies of knowledge, or names of sciences. It comes from the Greek word '*logos*', which means the word or explanation, account, or narrative. Examples of English words formed from *logos* are logic, dialogue, and monologue, all of which have something to do with the word. When a new theory or branch of knowledge emerges to warrant further research, English forms new words by adding '-logy' to the field, meaning 'study of', for example psychology, sociology, cosmology, and so on.

The complete word, '*scenology*', does not currently exist in the English dictionary, and I am using it here to describe an emerging body of knowledge that is rooted in Africa and the diaspora around the notion of African perform-ance practice. 'Afroscenology' refers to performance practices developed by African practitioners and Africanists, which respond to the African playing cultures by incorporating their performance traditions, forming work that is unique to Africa and its diaspora. The description of this work through its theoretical tenets provides grounds for the formulation of a theory, which I have called 'Afroscenology'. Afroscenology is not only a theory, but a mode of thought and action, a body knowledge that is still growing, which seeks to document, conceptualise, and analyse the ways African practitioners and Africanists write, perform, creatively make, direct, design, and vocalise their work. The training of performers and writers already exists in the various theatre companies in Africa, which specialise in community and workshop theatre. This knowledge has not yet fully percolated into African university curricula. Afroscenology, as a branch of knowledge, seeks to expand the domain of performer training by tapping into this tacit knowledge, which currently resides in various theatre companies, and formalise it through documentation and teaching in the formal education sector.

This is not just a pipe dream. At the University of the Witwatersrand, under the programme of decolonisation, I have overseen a rapid process of changing the training of performers in the Department of Theatre and Performance by incorporating African modes of performance, which fellow colleagues currently call Black aesthetics. We have made several changes to the naming of courses and the content subsumed in those courses. We changed from 'dramatic art' to 'theatre and performance', and dropped acting from our vocabulary. We replaced this with performance practice for Years 1 and 2, and performance studies for Years 3 and 4. The various changes that have taken place under my stewardship will be a lengthy discussion for another paper. Suffice it to say, several colleagues who worked in the workshop theatre tradition have now joined the university and are developing a performing and writing training curriculum, which they are using in the studios. This material and the discoveries they are making in the studios have become the subject of research for their higher degrees.

Some Examples of Arts Research in Pursuit of an African Aesthetic

Before the phase of arts research began in Africa, theatre-makers responded to colonial models in a variety of ways, which Frantz Fanon (1963b) called a literature of assimilation to the metropolis models, followed by a literature of just before the battle, which told African stories in borrowed western aesthetics, and, finally, a literature of combat that fought western models, both aesthetically and in terms of content. After these three phases, African scholars began a new phase of researching and experimentation through creative practice to establish a national theatre aesthetic or an African one. The first recorded arts research was by Herbert Dhlomo, who wrote several plays and theorised his practice. After studying the various performance modes of the Zulu, he called this African theatre '*izibongelo*', which he defined as 'all forms of tribal dramatic art' (Dhlomo, 1939, p. 48).

In 1960, a new political and cultural movement called the Black Consciousness Movement emerged and began a theatre programme in 1972, which Steve Biko, the thinktank of the movement, called 'Black theatre' (2004, p. 98). The aesthetics of theatre can be picked from several plays that were written and performed under its banner, such as Mthuli ka Shezi's *Shanti* (1981). Its focus was not so much the form but the message. Mafika Gwala, another active theorist of the Black theatre movement, described the aesthetic as African national theatre (Gwala, 1973). What is significant here is the desire to create a continental aesthetic that would carry the weight and depth of African experiences. The Ghanaian arts researcher, Mohammed Ben Abdallah, calls this African aesthetic in the Akan language '*Abibigoro*', meaning 'black theatre or theatre of African people' (cited in Asiedu, 2011). Black theatre scholars who described the same theatre used either term: Black theatre or African theatre. What is clear from the foregoing descriptive epithets is an attempt since 1939 to describe and name the African aesthetic.

In 1976, Ngũgĩ wa Thiong'o together with Kimani Gecau and Ngũgĩ wa Mĩriĩ, at the prompting by the Kamiriithu community, started an arts research project by the same name, Kamiriithu theatre. They worked with untrained villagers and workers to create a workshop play called *Ngaahika Ndeenda* (*I will marry when I want*) (1977). After the project, wa Thiong'o reflected thereon based on what he had learnt from the villagers, who he saw as the custodians of his mother tongue, Gikuyu, and African culture. *Ngaahika Ndeenda* was an example of African theatre and wa Thiong'o began to theorise his practice using the term 'African theatre' to describe his aesthetic. The tenets of this theatre resonate with Efua Sutherland's *Anansegoro* (loosely translated as 'Spider' play), epitomised by her production, *The Marriage of Anansewa* (1975). In this play, she demonstrates how the African storytelling tradition can be used as a technique to write and perform an African play. All the descriptors speak to a common aesthetic developed at different times across the African continent. Based on their artistic practice, they have argued that this form may be deployed in theatre-making in Africa and have demonstrated its applicability and efficacy in their respective plays. I want to posit this form as the first tenets of Afroscenology. However, in as much as it is an alternative to western theatre, it does not necessarily negate any useful elements from the western tradition, albeit they may never take the dominant position in the hierarchy of signs.

In African art, the storytelling tradition has not only influenced African theatre, but also African novels and films. For much of African theatre that subscribes to the basic tenets of Afroscenology, the 'opening' is characterised by a common quality: *nhanganyaya/ukuvula* (Shona and Nguni, respectively). Sam Ukala has called the beginning, the 'law of opening' (Ukala, 2001, p. 33). The storyteller/*sarungano* (Shona), which may be played by one person or shared by several people, enters the space and introduces the story by telling it to the audience and introducing the other characters. In Ben Abdallah's *The Slaves* (2005), for example, the storytellers/*sarungano* are played by a group of people: a search party pursuing captured slaves. They perform a poetry of abuse at the audience. When the *sarungano* is played by several people, the style of performance becomes what is called, in Swahili, a '*ngonjera*'. The various plays mentioned here deploy the *ngonjera* performance technique, which the western gaze may read as a chorus. However, in the African sense, the *sarungano* take turns to deliver the narrative, and sometimes take the lines together in choral chants. In the western sense, a chorus denotes part of drama sung or spoken by the chorus and this includes the person who delivers the prologue and epilogue or group of people in a play who perform segments of drama simultaneously. In the African sense, this tradition is derived from Nguni *izimbongi* or West African griots or East African *ngonjera*. These performers are more on the side of poets than singers. The performance codes are underpinned by tradition, are more ecstatic, louder, performative and fall on the side of bards than chorus or rather a combination of bards and chorus depending on the content.

In my artistic research, I tested this theory through staging the classic play, *Oedipus Rex* (c. 429 BC), which I adapted to *Vumani Oedipus* (2015). I used a group of praise singers, termed in Nguni, '*izimbongi*', to introduce the story by singing a song of suffering. The king's chief of staff, *ndunankulu,* also played the part of the *sarungano* by addressing the king and the audience, explaining why they were gathered and what the state needed to do. The combination of *izimbongi* and *ndunankulu* provided a pivotal vehicle to deliver the story and add commentary from time to time. Fatima Dike deploys the same technique in her play, *Sacrifice for Kreli* (1978), when a group of male *izimbongi* deliver praises to King Kreli, according to Xhosa custom, and provide commentary on the behaviour of men who occupied two different ideological positions: surrendering to the British or fighting them.

This theoretical tenet is not only applicable to African-generated playtexts but, like any other theory, can be deployed to any play-text. The artist-researcher who put it to test several times, Ben Abdallah, concluded that the *ngonjera* technique 'is a tool of the director. I see myself taking any play, written [. . .] and doing it in the *abibigoro* style [Afroscenology style] without changing the play, talk about the author and then the play begins. Then, at certain points, he cuts into the action and comments on it' (cited in Asiedu, 2011, p. 372).

The second theoretical tenet of Afroscenology is *visiosonic* dramaturgy. The neologism suggests a combination that is visual and auditory. All over the African continent, song and dance form an integral part of social life and playing culture. Arts researchers like Fatima Dike, Ngũgĩ wa Thiong'o, Mohammed Ben Abdallah, and Stephen Chifunyise have reached one conclusion that work deploying the theory of Afroscenology will have song and dance (*nziyo/ingoma* and *kudzana/tshibilika* in Shona and Ndebele, respectively). In a typical western play deploying the six elements of Aristotle's dramatic theory (plot, character, thought, language, melody, and spectacle), language with pleasurable accessories (*lexis*) will be a key component. Language will subsume elements like poetic language, emotion, diction, silence, beats, thoughts, units, and subtext. While Africanists and African theatre-makers may choose to use language in their performances, which may or may not have some of the Aristotelian elements, the Afroscenological near equivalent of language is broader than that provided by Aristotle. Wa Thiong'o has called this category 'the language of African theatre' (1986, p. 34), which subsumes song, dance, and mime. These three languages of African theatre, in the case of wa Thiong'o et al.'s *Maitu Njugira* (Mother Sing for Me; 1982), were more dominant than the spoken word (*lexis*) as he asserts, 'dance, mime, song were more dominant than words in telling the story of repression and resistance. The visual and sound images carried the burden of the narrative and the analysis' (1986, p. 58).

Stephen Chifunyise, theorising on what called 'national theatre' (1986, p. 35), a form of new theatre that he wanted the newly independent Zimbabwe to adopt in 1980, makes several interesting observations about the place of song and dance. In this regard, Chifunyise proposes two ways of creating theatre. The first proposal is centred on appropriating the western dramaturgical frame and then grafting it with African texts. Here, the theatre-maker takes recourse to making theatre following a linear plot but incorporates song and dance at strategic points as summarised in Chifunyise's training manual.

- In every break in the play
- At change of scenes/acts
- To create an atmosphere/location/cultural environment or indicate progression of time
- To bring life into the play
- To explain or expand the theme of the play/remind the audience of the message/hidden theme
- To involve or awaken the audience
- To begin or end the play/rejuvenate it/help to create impact

In this approach, the matrix of performance is western, and indigenous texts are inscribed within that matrix, and they alter the western dramaturgical frame while indigenous texts are themselves equally altered.

Chifunyise's second proposal may aptly be described as 'de-dramatisation' of theatre, in the sense that he attempts to move away from the primacy of the written text, implying the death of the playwright and the ascendancy of the director in the creative process, to a type of theatre that utilises the body as the nucleus of performance or, as he puts it, as 'the most critical tool in creating theatre' (1997, p. ii). Chifunyise describes this theatre as 'dance-drama', although the term itself is a misnomer in the sense that, in actual performance of this theatre, drama is almost dead. Dialogue is minimal, and where it is used, it is not intended to be constructed around the Aristotelian notion of plot. Instead, the theatre-maker creates a performance through dance, song, music, mime, chants, ululation, recitals, and movement. According to Chifunyise, the theatre-maker could bring traditional songs, dances and ceremonies, rallies, recitals, and festivals to the stage as they are, and then rearrange them for coherence and order. This seems to resonate with the Caribbean theatre of exuberance or theatre of assimilation proposed by Errol Hill (see Balme, 1999). Since Chifunyise believes in the functionality of theatre and its ideological impact, he proposes that the songs and dances chosen by the theatre-maker should depict the interests of peasants and workers (1986). Alternatively, Chifunyise proposes that the songs and dances could be used out of their original contexts by changing the words and inscribing new ones to an existing melody. The traditional dances could be re-choreographed to suit the new needs of the director.

Related to the elements of song and dance is mime. What I seek to establish is to foreground mime as a tenet of Afroscenology. This kind of mime is not to be confused with the western tradition associated with Jacques Lecoq. This mime is different and is called *kuyedzesera/ukunyenyeza* in Zimbabwe and South Africa, respectively. These words mean to try to be someone or something in the absence of the object or person. This 'attempt to be' is not limited to physical means but incorporates sound action produced by the human body. Thus, the body is capable of performing or expressing anything. Based on the duality of the process, which is both physical and aural, I would call the technique *Afrosonic* mime to distinguish it from the classical mime. This concept is fully developed in Section 4.

Take, for instance, the performance of Fatima Dike's *Sacrifice for Kreli* (1976). King Kreli is planning a sacrifice to his ancestors to ascertain whether he should go back to Bomvanaland (a land now conquered and taken over by the British) to fight the British or to bring the Galeka women and children to the valley to stay with their families, as opposed to being the subjects of the British. Fourteen men performed the ritual. It involved standing around a kraal (mimed) and identifying an acceptable bull amongst a big herd of cattle (mimed). The performers drive the herd by way of producing bellowing sounds, whistling, shouting, and talking to animals. The herd is mimed through sounds. In its 1976 run, Rob Amato, the producer and co-director with Makwedini Mtsaka, remembers the mime as follows,

> [...] and at the end of the first act there are fourteen people bringing the imaginary beast in, which always got ovations. There are fourteen people in a coordinated mime, which was rehearsed with me being the bull, and they would bring me down, while I put all the resistance, I could master, just to get the right muscular tensions of the act. Five men at each of my arms, and of course, I would go down [...] Anywhere, they put it to the ground, and it falls with a great thump as it lands, and this is done by an actor, you know. You've got so many actors that you don't know who's doing the sound effects. Then

the king passes the spear between the bull's legs and up and down the body, and then stabs it and one of the actor's cues—you can't tell which, they're all bending down holding this thing, kneeling and holding it, and there is a lot of noise. (Solberg, 1999, p. 59)

Read together with the stage directions in the play, the fourteen performers together try to create an atmosphere and ambience to convince the audience that they are driving a herd of cattle through human and animal sounds, and, of course, using their hands to suggest whips and spears. They do not try to be animals, but they produce sounds that create an atmosphere for suspending disbelief. Since mime is not scripted, there is a greater tendency for the aleatory technique to be used, which Ukala calls 'free enactment' (2001, p. 36). Ukala uses this epithet to describe the ability of the performer to imitate actions and speech of a character or non-human object without being fully psychological. It also involves the element of bifurcation: the ability to play multiple characters by shifting from one to the other in quick succession, including playing inanimate objects. While this is rehearsed, the performance changes each night depending on the activities of the assemblage. The subject of *Afrosonic* mime is an essay-length discussion on its own; here, I just want to demonstrate how it works in the context of Afroscenology theory.

Why Artistic Research in Africa?

Michel Foucault (1980) argues that power does not weaken and vanish. It can retreat, but it has the propensity to re-organise its forces and reinvent itself in another form, pursuing the same objectives. Within the postcolony, the lost power can be channelled more rigorously in the academy and the field of artistic production. Coloniality is an invisible power structure that sustains colonialism and its unequal relations of exploitation and domination even after the end of colonialism. Within the academy, there is cognitive domination, which ensures that inequality reproduces itself. The modes of knowledge production and dissemination in South African, historically white, universities are largely Eurocentric.

- The curriculum will prescribe more western plays for staging, studying, and criticism than African ones.
- The training of performers will use western methods (e.g., the psycho-technique and its various versions like Chekhov, Mesmer, Alexander, Strasberg, Grotowski, Spolin, Mamet, etc.) and, as an afterthought, one Asian technique and side lined African performer training methods.
- The curriculum may privilege western theatre history and theatre innovators and neglect African theatre history.

- The curriculum may chronologically study western theories; naturalism, realism, modernism (symbolism, Dadaism, futurism, epic, expressionism, etc.) postmodernism, and so on, and neglect African ones; Negritudism, Pan-Africanism, Afrocentricity, Afro-futurism, Afroscenology, Womanism (an African version of feminism), etc.
- Ali Mazrui has called this 'Euro-heroism' by which he means 'the tendency toward giving disproportionate attention to European and western achievements in arts' (2009, p. xi).
- 'Euro-exclusivity'. In terms of knowledge production, disproportionate space is given to the western side of theatre history and, in the case of South Africa, white theatre history and the role whites have played in advancing South African theatre.

The armed struggle was the first phase of decolonisation. In almost all postcolonies, students were the first to reject a colonial curriculum: Zimbabwe in the 1980s, Kenya in the late 1960s, and South Africa from 2015. Artistic research has the potential to decolonise the curriculum in Africa. Emanating from the seven approaches to artistic research, I conclude that more artistic research may invariably lead to the production of new plays/performances from the African context that may be used by students and researchers for their courses and research. As the process gathers momentum and artist-researcher document their practice, it will lead to production of new performer training methods and techniques that speak to the African context, e.g., Afroscenology and Afro-futurism. The world may benefit from Africa. Finally, this praxis will challenge the *logos,* which is the bedrock of western episteme. The western academy has always worshipped positivist ways of producing episteme while at the same time demeaning the knowledge gained through making, performing, and creating. Arts research challenges the dictatorship of *logos* and privileges embodied ways of knowing a major – paradigm shift.

3 Rombic Theatre: Celebrating the Fools of Africa and Crafting a Theory

I want to focus on plays that feature stories and characters that have survived calamities. Diseases hit hardest the African continent as its healthcare facilities are incomparably weaker to the rest of the world. Natural disasters also hit hardest the African continent as its preparedness to mitigate their effects is not as advanced as the western world. Violent conflicts to decolonise, to resolve ethnic differences, to control resources and some of them sponsored by western governments have affected the African continent more than any other place in the world (perhaps what is looming in Europe sparked by the Russo-Ukraine conflict might surpass the record). Several plays have emerged in the African continent which feature stories and characters who have survived some of these misfortunes. These characters appear to be not mentally stable and may be struggling with a physical ailment, whatever form it may take. The characters may be social or economic outcasts who may have left normal society and are living in the streets, woods, squatter camps, or any such place not deemed decent for human habitation. The plays themselves are post-linear and postrealist. When studying or watching these plays it may be tempting to link them to the western absurd theatre tradition and deploy its theory to make sense of them. Soon we realise that the plays do not obey its tenets to the letter. The usual condescending Hamitic hypothesis that nothing happens in Africa unless it is influenced by others is then mobilised with such conclusions that this African tradition is a poor imitation of western absurd theatre. Of course, diseases and calamities are not a preserve of one part of the world; they occur all over the world allowing artists to respond to them in particular ways. What this section seeks to do is to delink this type of theatre from the western absurd theatre and reconnect it to the known African playing culture. I seek to re-language the practice by proffering the term *Rombic Theatre* to describe the African tradition. I will then discuss its nature and occurrence and allow the theory to emerge from this process.

All theory comes from practice and comes back to guide practice. Aristotle did not propound the dramatic theory from nothing. He studied the work of his contemporaries including Aristophanes, Sophocles, and Euripides and discovered certain commonalities in the plays which he reduced to six elements – plot (*mythos*), character (*ethos*), thought (*dianoia*), language/diction (*lexis*), melody (*melos*), and spectacle (*opsis*). To define Afroscenology, we can look at the works of African theatre-makers to establish the theatric theory (the form of the text) which is to be distinguished from the Afro-technique, a performatic theory. A play is called *mutambo/umdlalo* in Shona and Nguni, respectively. The same words are used to refer to games, rituals, ceremonies, and cultural performances. I find them more inclusive than drama. I propose to use the term theatric theory (*mutambo/umdlalo*) to refer to the elements that go to make the play and the play itself is a theatrical text as opposed to a dramatic text. I am using the term theatrical text in the same manner Christopher Balme (1999) uses it to mean any kind of textual blueprint that is intended for or attains performance. A theatrical text is broader than a dramatic text which follows an Aristotelian linear structure. A theatrical text includes any text that pre-exists a performance or comes after a performance that may take any form and structure. A theatric theory is a term I use to describe the tenets and form of such texts and is used to distinguish it from its western cousin, the dramatic theory.

My theory is based on experimental works that were developed in laboratories pursuing the noble goals of developing African theatre such as arts researchers who experimented using university resources like Wole Soyinka, Ngugi wa Thiong'o, Hussein Abraham, Robert Kavanagh Mshengu, John Clarke, Ola Rotimi and my own practice in South Africa. From this African great tradition, I want to distinguish between two types of African theatre practice – epic theatre and *rombic* theatre. I shall return to the latter shortly. African epic theatre refers to a production that relies on ancient oral performance texts such as griotic narratives, legendary/mythical stories, praise poetry (*izibongo*), rituals, ceremonies, epic poems, songs dances, and new performance forms developed in the African townships of the many urban centres that emerged in Africa. There are two versions of epic theatre; the first one is a large-scale production and requires a comparatively big budget to mount it. It relies on an orchestra of musicians and dancers playing various instruments. In the absence of these, the director may choose to play pre-recorded music. The dancers perform the text and sing. Examples of plays that come to mind include Credo Mutwa's *uNosilimela* (1981), Ngugi wa Thiong'o's *Devil on the Cross* (2018) (adaptation), *I Will Marry When I Want* (1982), Robert Mshengu Kavanagh's *Mavambo* (1997b), and *Hamba Kahle MK* (2019), John. P Clarke's *Ozidi* (1966). The second version of epic theatre deploys the same techniques as the first but utilises the human body to generate the performance without any recourse to instruments and dense scenography. Performers range from one to about five. Examples include Ngema, Mtwa, and Simon's *Woza Albert*, Mhlanga's *Workshop Negative* (1992), Foot's *Tshepang* (2005), Fugard's *Sizwe Bansi is Dead* (1972), Gcina Mhlophe's *Have you seen Zandile* (2002), and Kavanagh's *Workshop '71 plays* (2016a). In both versions, the elements of theatric theory (*mutambo/umdlalo*)[1] include *vatambi/abadlali*[2] (players), mime, song, dance, and *matambiro* (playing culture).

Aristotle uses the term character to describe the fictional human beings who populate the play in his dramatic theory. Character presupposes that the actor will try as much as is possible to imitate the actions of another person to become character. The term, character, will be inappropriate to describe a player in epic theatre. The *mutambi/umdlali*[3] in epic theatre will, indeed, at some points, become character, but will get out of character to sing and dance. When the latter happens, the *mutambi/umdlali* is playing himself/herself and clearly does not become character. Most African languages in Southern Africa do not use the term actor, but player, for example, *modiragatsi* (role player) in Tswana,

---

[1] Noun in singular form to refer to a play.   [2] Noun in plural form to refer to players.
[3] Noun in singular form to refer to a player.

sebapali/sebapadi (player) in southern Sesotho, and *moraloke* (player) in Northern Sesotho/Sepedi. The term 'performer' rather than actor best describes this sort of playing. The Aristotelian character develops as a single entity interacting with other characters. By the end of the play, the character would have developed to become a changed person. In African epic theatre, any attempt at character is destabilised by bifurcation. The *mutambi/umdlali* transforms into other players including non-human performants but returning to the leitmotif player.

Rombic Theatre and Characters

I now return to the second formation of African theatre. *Rombe* is a Shona word to describe a person who has withdrawn from normal society and is in the habit of strolling and wandering about stopping when followed by a crowd to perform poetry, a musical instrument, or some intelligent, esoteric sayings. In ancient times and even after colonial occupation, characters like these would move from village to village performing their skill. Parents became warry of their children if they were found trying to learn to play a musical instrument as this would lead, in some cases, to these children abandoning farming and family and start wandering around performing their gift and receiving a few food rewards. Since they have no fixed aboard, they are considered as vagrant, tramp, loafer, or vagabond. Early Zimbabwean musicians like Thomas Mapfumo, Oliver Mtukudzi, and Ephat Mujuru recount the pressure which they faced from their parents when they chose to pursue musical careers. Their parents opposed their chosen careers as, in their generation, gifted musicians would become *marombe* roaming around without purpose. Northern Shona uses the word *fuza* to describe the same person, albeit this one is more specific to a person who is deficient of understanding. Synonyms include *mboko, dununu, dinga, dofo, mupengo,* and *benzi. Mboko* in ancient Zimbabwean times referred to court fools who were part of the Mwene Mutapa entourage to entertain the emperor with dances, wise sayings, and foolery. All these words are descriptors of various forms of mental deficiency and the personalities referred to belong to the *romboids*. I use *romboids* as a neologism to describe a category of personalities that belongs to the mentally deficient, lacking judgement and wisdom. The *marombe* were also very active in communal gatherings for purposes of performing rituals, dancing, cultural performance, and ceremonies to a point where Africans have recorded their role in a proverb. '*Benzi nderako kudzana unopururudza*'/a moron still belongs to his family and when he dances, the mother will cheer him by ululating.

The closest example of a *rombe* would be a court fool, an important character in Shakespearean tragedy and comedy. This tradition of *rombic* theatre or a performance involving *romboids* is not just a Zimbabwean practice; it was widespread in southern Africa in precolonial times. In 1586, a Portuguese explorer/trader, Friar Joao Dos Santos, visited a Chope royal court in what is today, Mozambique (at that time a part of the Mwene Mutapa Kingdom) and saw the *rombe* players in action. Describing the actions at the court, he recorded 'the king (...) has another class of Kaffir [*sic*] who are called *marombes* [*sic*], which means the same as jester, and who sang, shouted praises, told jokes and performed acrobatics' (cited in Coplan, 1987, p. 11). David Coplan recorded the same tradition being prevalent in South Africa in the 1900s where the *rombe* performers played at dance competitions. The tradition had appropriated European top hats and tailcoats as costume that they wore for comic purposes. What Dos Santos saw them do at the king's court, they did the same to European mine bosses by way of jokes, satiric praises, and acrobatics at organised dance competitions.

In its original meaning, *marombe* meant destitute vagrants who were hired by kings to entertain him at his court. The term is associated with entertainment. In other Bantu languages which use an 'L' for 'R' dancers have been given the name, *malombe*, especially in Kalanga. Since dancing is always performed with music/song, the Venda, an extension of Kalanga and Shona, have developed a musical genre called *malombo* and have brought honour to the term by even naming musical bands using the term, for example Malombo Jazz Maker, a group that was popular in South Africa in the 1960s credited for popularising the *Malombe* music. The music was developed from Venda indigenous healing practices (Davhula, 2015). The healing practice is called *malombo* while those who have been healed before through the ritual of singing and dancing are called *malombe*, a semantic which is not far off from its ancient meaning of wandering destitute musicians.

I have taken time to describe the *romboids* to argue the fact that Africa has a growing body of work that is deploying these characters to tell stories. In the majority of plays, the characters are people of colour, Africoids with a few possible exceptions where Caucasoids created from the agency of African playwrights or Africanists also feature in some of the plays, for example, Ravengai's *Trauma Centre* (2001) and Marechera's *The Alley*. The plays that feature *romboids* are Dambudzo Marechera's *The Alley* (1994b), *Killwatch* (1994a), Wole Soyinka's *Madmen and Specialists* (1971), *The Road* (1965), *The Swamp Dwellers* (1973), Athol Fugard's *Boesman and Lena* (1983), Andrew Whaley's *The Rise and Shine and Comrade Fiasco* (1991), Ola Rotimi's *Holding Talks* (1979), and Zakes Mda's *We Shall Sing for the Fatherland* (1993). Soyinka's *The Swamp Dwellers* presents a character who is a *romboid*, called Beggar (1964b). After a famine in the north of Nigeria, the blind beggar decides to travel south by following a river in the hope that where the river meets the sea, he would find land to till. He has lost track of time. Throughout the journey he relies on the benevolence of various people he meets who give him food and money. When he finally reaches the south at Makuri and Alu's homestead, he begs to become Igwezu's (Makuri's son) bondservant so that he could till land for him. Igwezu breaches the social norm by blaspheming against the local religious leader, Kadiye, who represents the serpent god of fertility and rain. He has to return to the city to escape Kadiye's vengeance. Beggar begs to go with Igwezu to the city. He has become a *rombe*, a wanderer indeed. In Marechera's *The Alley*, the main characters, Rhodes and Robin, are of the *rombe* type as they have left their homes and opted to live on the streets of Harare.

The history of criticism has taught us that when an African work of art has been classified as an overseas extension of a western prototype, it must conform to all the tenets of absurd theatre and if does not, then analysts will condemn it as a poor imitation. Regrettably, the work has been classified as absurd theatre even by some African commentators (Acholonu, 1984; Ebewo, 2008). Zakes Mda makes a revealing statement that by the time he wrote his play *We Shall Sing for the Fatherland* which Rob Amato classified as Dadaism he had never read any of the absurdist theatre and therefore its influence was unlikely. In fact, Rob Amato, in an introduction to a collection of Zakes Mda's plays entitled *Fools, Bells, and The Habit of Eating*, calls Mda's style of writing 'Mdadaism' to refer to the possible influence of Dadaism to Mda's writing. Mda contests this perception.

It is Marvin Carlson (2003) who argues that theatre is 'ghosted' or 'haunted' by previous stories, forms, buildings, sets, and techniques which it recycles in new innovative ways. In other words, the DNA of old theatre practices are found in contemporary performances combined with new discoveries and, in some cases, transnational influences. I propose here that *rombic* theatre is haunted by indigenous African texts, language (in its broader sense), and characters which it appropriates to realise a new theatre. In the field of African poetry, there is a style of poetry that is performed to entertain the audience. In most cases, there is no message, but a series of statements that are so humorous that audience members had to bring belts/ropes to tie their ribs (*sungai mabvu*) to protect themselves from rib ache caused by too much laughter. This kind of writing can exist in poetry or prose or even dramatic form. Moderkai Hamutyinei collected and transformed some of these stories into a collection of three plays which he titled *Sungai Mbabvu/Tie your Ribcage* (1973). In Shona, this poetry, prose, or play is called *ndyaringo*. *Rombic* theatre recycles *ndyaringo* that manifest as clever and/or comedic sayings during verbal interchange. Related to *ndyaringo* is a verbal exchange game called *zvinemero/ukuphoxana* in Shona and Ndebele, respectively. Boys normally play the verbal exchange game where two players choose to engage in verbal insults while others listen and enjoy the insults (*zvituko/iziphoxo*). There is no story development at all. The exchanges can be high pitched but will not change the circumstances of the players. There may be a great deal of laughter but there is no plot development. Similarly, *rombic* dialogue, consistent with its insults origins, does not move the story forward. It is meant to while up time in a moment that is entertaining and beautiful to watch.

There is a type of indigenous theatre from which *rombic* theatre draws its characters and form. Victor Turner (1988) calls this theatre, social drama. I want to give an example from a Zimbabwean context which begins with what Turner calls 'breach of norm'. In most African patriarchal societies, women are protected by invoking the wrath of the gods on any man who is implicated in causing their pain. The worst breach of norm a son can commit is to hurt his mother physically or emotionally. In order to atone his sins, he must play a fool, in the fashion of a *rombe*, by wearing a sackcloth and applying white ashes all over his body. He must move from one household to another with a sack begging for small grain. At each household, he is scorned by everybody and released after a small portion of grain has been put into his sack. When he has gathered enough and of course enduring all the insults of the village, he uses the grain to brew beer that the patriarchs will use to perform a ritual for his forgiveness and reintegration into the community. This social drama is called *kutandabotso* in Shona. Wole Soyinka's *Strong Breed* (1964a) relies on this notion of social drama for its story.

A further antecedent to *rombic* theatre is the tradition of announcing. It can be either a solo art or an art form that is performed in front of an audience. When it is a solo art, the announcer is advertising an important event to his community such as the maturation of a traditional brew. Traditional beer takes at least five days to mature. On the fifth day, quite early in the morning before villagers have awoken to do any chores, the announcer takes to an anthill or a hill and delivers a flamboyant speech about the sumptuous beer. Rapoko products are considered more delicate than sorghum, millet, or maize. The announcer creates a poem about the ingredients and the many beautiful women who will come to enjoy the drink. He may mention the meal that may be served with beer and implores the neighbours to tell one another by mentioning their praise names.

The solo performance may be what is called *kurova bembera*, loosely translated to megaphone diplomacy. When an unpleasant happening has occurred in the village and the responsible person is assumed to be a resident of the village, the head of the family or his nominee will do the same as the beer announcer and launch a tirade of attacks on the culprit without mentioning their name. He warns him not to continue with the antisocial behaviour. The poetry may bring great joy to the innocent while the words will hit hard on the culprit. The diction may resemble the *zvituko/Iziphoxo* except there will be no 'return fire', in this instance. We find these long speeches in the following plays like Soyinka's *Swamp Dwellers* and *The Trails of Brother Jero*, Fugard's *Boesman and Lena*, and several others.

The other source of *rombic* theatre is the theatre of war. Actuality, in some cases, in Africa resembles theatre. With a few possible exceptions, especially those countries which were protectorates of western colonial masters, nearly all African countries went to war to liberate themselves from colonial rule. It is from this theatre of war that some African playwrights of the *rombic* theatre genre have derived their characters and stories. The consequences of war reflect on the survivors' bodies by way of scars, missing body parts, damaged body parts, projectiles still embedded in survivors' bodies, and psychological deformities. The latter reflects in the minds of survivors through post-traumatic disorders which manifest in different ways in different survivors. Frantz Fanon, the writer of the seminal book, *The Wretched of the Earth* (1963a), was a psychiatrist by training and he devoted an entire chapter 'colonial war and mental disorders' to record many cases he dealt with during Algeria's war of independence ranging from impotence, homicidal impulsions, psychosis, stupor, aneroid symptoms, nightmares, sadism, accusatory delirium, suicidal conduct, neurosis, puerperal psychosis, affective intellectual modifications, motor instability, nervous depression, cenesthopathies, phobias, verbal stereotypy, inhibition, nephritic colic, menstruation trouble in women, and so on. During Zimbabwe's liberation war, Rhodesian forces made occasional raids into liberation forces bases in Mozambique and Zambia. One such attack was in Chimoio, Mozambique in 1977, during Operation Dingo. After three days of Rhodesian aggression, ZANLA soldiers began the process of retrieving bodies and burying them. According to Mutambara (2014) on two occasions, the first one involving eight soldiers, fighters began to be hysterical acting as if they were possessed and speaking in strange languages. They were tearing their clothes and destroying their weapons. On the second occasion, fifty six soldiers developed similar symptoms, but these ones jumped into two mass graves where their comrades were being buried and spoke in unintelligible languages (Mutambara, 2014, pp. 192–196). These stories are just a glimpse into what was to unfold when the war was over in 1980. Being a survivor of the war myself, I saw these ex-soldiers struggling with different kinds of ailments which prompted me to write my play, *Trauma centre*. Andrew Whaley's *The Rise and Shine of Comrade Fiasco* relies on the same experiences creating a genre of theatre which I call here *rombic* theatre, on account of its reliance on *marombe* characters. Dambudzo Marechera's play, *The alley*, is based on characters who were soldiers during Zimbabwe's war of independence. In the writing of *The Alley* (1994b) and *Killwatch* (1994a), Marechera relied on his own life, living in the streets of Harare as a *rombe*/tramp. There, he met with all kinds of people, including mentally deranged ex-Rhodesian soldiers and ex-guerrilla fighters. Some of the ex-guerrilla fighters, suffering from post-traumatic disorders were being rehabilitated in a nearby African township called Ruwa. The two plays were based on his own life and that of other *romboids* he had met in the streets. If content determines form, can anyone lay claim to the resultant form that emerges when *rombic* characters interact with one another? For the theatre practice that utilises *romboids*, I am proposing the term *rombic* theatre to describe it.

Rombe characters are deformed, aged, deranged, or social invalids. My own play, *Trauma Centre*, captures the lives of three male survivors of the Zimbabwean war of liberation. One of the survivors is Zeppelin who fought on the side of liberation forces. He has bullets and shrapnel embedded in his body making walking a nightmare. He is a stiff man who walks on crutches. He suffers from psychosomatic disorders characterised by moderate loss of memory. He, however, remembers extremely traumatic events which happened in the past. He is irritable and is given to seeking solitude and hating conversations. The second character is Reito who fought on the side of Rhodesian security forces during Zimbabwe's war of independence. He suffers from insomnia which gives him nocturnal uproars. Because of this illness, he has a wholesale aggressivity which lingers around but is more prominent when his illness spikes. He hallucinates and blabbers incoherently when his illness reaches peak levels. In this state, he acts as if he is possessed. A possessed person contorts and convulses. The spirit has a noticeable physical impact on the body. The third character is Themba who is a born free but survived political violence of the liberation war. He has a fresh scar on his head which is covered by a bandage. Clearly, based on the descriptions aforementioned, *rombe* characters are sufferers, and suffering tends to leave a permanent mask on their faces. Wole Soyinka's *The Road, Madmen and Specialists,* and *The Swamp Dwellers* demonstrate features of *rombe* characters where pain, decay, and age as physiological features haunt these characters. In *The Road*, Murano who is supposed to tutor the professor is blind. In *Madmen and Specialists*, a blind person is the protagonist, and in *The Swamp Dwellers*, a visually impaired beggar from the north is employed as a metaphor for wisdom.

The title of the play, *Trauma Centre,* is both the setting and a metaphor of chaos, *chirombe* (the quality or state of being a wandering vagrant) and bondage. A hospital as a setting immediately strikes one with associations of disease – psychotic and physical trauma. This metaphor of disease is used frequently in African playwrighting. In Fugard's *Boesman and Lena*, the old Xhosa man, Outa, has a strange disease which takes his life before the play comes to an end. In Whaley's *The Rise and Shine of Comrade Fiasco*, Fiasco is deranged and given to living in the mountain caves as a *rombe* for eight years. He has psychosomatic disorders, speaks in gibberish and fears speech. When he tries to speak, he does so in monosyllables or in extended incoherent statements. He gets hysterical when interrogated. His nemesis, Chidhina, has a choleric temper and similarly suffers from post-traumatic disorders of the agoraphobia type. He has moderate loss of memory and cannot remember Comrade Fiasco, even though they fought together in the same detachment during the liberation war in Zimbabwe. In fact, all the characters in the play are social outcasts as they are housed in a state prison. The same metaphor of derangement is used by Soyinka in *The Strong Breed*. The play celebrates fools (*marombe*). One of the fools is Ifada who it appears is a personal aid of Eman, the main character. Like Outa in *Boesman and Lena*, he does not have the logos. He is present from the beginning of the play to the end but without speaking a single word. His origins are unknown, and his disease is also unknown. The second *rombe* in the play is a character simply identified as Girl. She has an affliction of unknown names or origin. Her source of action is derived from collecting clothes and building an effigy so that she could present this ritual object at the festival of the new year lasting the whole night. She hopes that when the new year arrives, her curses which afflict her would be taken away from her and she would live a normal life. By the end of the play, her circumstances have not changed. The rest of the characters in the play are normal. In all these examples, disease is anti-human; it brings rot, decadence, and death to society. In addition to this focus on disease or madness as metaphor, Trauma Centre hospital, the setting for my play, houses victims of trauma. In the words of Bradley et al.:

> Trauma indicates a caesura, necessitates a pause – it arises from a moment of rupture, of radical disjunction . . . it offends our belief in the link between the empirical knowledge and control, our aspiration to order, our assumptions of the logical, intelligible connection between cause and effect. Trauma fractures the fragile webs that provide the framework for our interface with social, political, cultural and emotional realms in which we function. (Bradley et al., 2001, p. 6)

Thise quotation accurately describes the condition of both Zeppelin and Reito in *Trauma Centre*. The word 'trauma' originates from Greek, meaning physical damage or wound, and this partly describes Zeppelin, who 'earned' some bullets and shrapnel in his pelvis during the war of independence. More frequently, however, trauma is used to denote a psychological state resulting from a particular event and this applies to Reito who is haunted by the shocking memories of his brutal methods of interrogating victims during the same war. How does the text represent such chaos? Reito and Zeppelin speak and act in a manner which does not respect logic or reason. When Reito gets a sudden shock, he does not respect the topic under discussion. He jumps to interrogating his victims and describes his battles with guerrillas. Time shifts from the present back to the past. When this shock recedes and Reito comes back to his quasi-normal condition, conversation continues with Zeppelin, but half the time they speak past each other. Communication between them ceases. These cracks and fissures in their speech mark spots where violence has occurred.

Based on my discussion of the sources of African plays, forthwith, I propose a theory of the African play through a diagrammatic representation.

In African playwrighting and possibly other cultures, the theatrical text is a product of a series of interlocking processes (see figure 1). Before it exists, there is a cultural text variously called a 'general text' (De Marinis, 1993), 'actuality' (Etherton, 1982), and 'playing culture' (Sauter, 2008). This text is not a homogenous one. It is composed of heterogeneous texts, such as mime, song, dance, philosophical episteme, ceremonies, rituals, cultural perform-ances, social drama and associated costume designs, body projects, prosthetics, and other texts that may be brought to bear on the theatrical text. The cultural text is the complex system of African performance culture, the entire collective of all its synchronous texts. When the playwright has experienced a creative compulsion and developed a concept she/he will choose which of the existing texts will be incorporated into the story which has to be constructed according to existing generic codes. I have established in this section that there are generic codes related to epic and *rombe* theatres. This is the domain of form, structure, performers/character, and style. Each culture has got its own theatrical

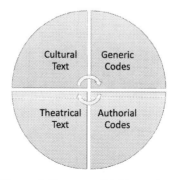

Figure 1 Sources of African plays

conventions relating to stage design and delivery style which determines the nature of dialogue to be used. If the play is going to be using griots or *izimbongi* (praise poets) or *ngonjera* (chorus), the conventions of these performances will be deployed in the writing of the play. Generic codes regulate the behaviour of characters/performers and invariably the manner the playwright will choose to construct them. Generic conventions include schools of thought, a movement such as the Black Theatre movement of the 1960s and 1970s, a genre; a style related to a historical period specific a culture-geographical region. Black Theatre conventions included the following: the message as form, dialogue of confrontation, use of Black techniques (idiom) in narratology, dealing with exclusively Black problems, directing the message to Black people to positively change their thinking, asserting Black people's dignity, rallying together around the concept of blackness, liberation philosophy, deploying African forms, values, and systems, and challenging old western concepts and values by offering alternatives developed from Black cultures. While other cultures have developed their generic codes to a point where they are now prescriptive by way of being institutionalised in the academy, socially acceptable and therefore used to make meaning of texts and performances (e.g., dramatic theory, Rasa theory, and Noh drama), in Africa this curriculumisation of the convention is still in the making. This section is part of that process. It is these codes that will assist the receptive process when reading or watching the play. The authorial codes are particular and distinctive to a playwright. They do not pre-exist, except in the creative faculties of the playwright. They only become visible after the play has been written. Each of the African playwrights who writes under the stamp of *rombic* theatre brings something unique that cannot be linked to the cultural or generic texts. Authorial codes act on both generic and cultural codes, transgressing them and creating something new. The denser these codes are in any work, the more the work will be proposing a new way of working that may become a theory in the future. Any creative output should have a certain level of authorial codes which we credit as creativity and contribution to the economy of creative knowledge. Since the codes are new, they will be experienced as difficult to decipher by any reader. The work is experienced as either under-coded or extra-coded or both.

Mwezva/Concertina Structure of African Playtexts

In African creativity, and I hope most cultures, everything begins from the cultural text that I have explained in the foregoing paragraph. In the African cultural text, the circle or semicircle is a key feature of design and it is associated with femininity and fertility. It is an opening that leads somewhere and for that

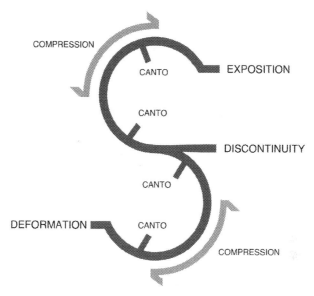

Figure 2 Circuitous structure of a theatrical text

reason it is considered female and fertile. The fecundity of the circle is from its ability to reproduce offspring. The traditional homestead is made up of a series of rondavels. Again, even if the head of the family is the husband, a homestead is gendered female since it belongs to a woman. In Shona idiom, this femininity is expressed in the proverb, '*musha mukadzi'*/a home is a home because of a woman. The ritual space is circular or semicircular. Archaeological findings have confirmed that ancient African cities were circular in formation, for example, the Great Zimbabwe monument and Mapungubwe. A quick Google check will reveal how the circle has inspired African fabric designs.

In a similar manner, African ceremonies, cultural performances, and rituals do not follow any rectilinear structure. Since African plays draw from this cultural text, they tend to favour the semicircular structure, and I have chosen to name the phases of this structure as exposition, compression 1, cantos, discontinuity, compression 2, cantos, and finally deformation as shown in Figure 2.[4]

The African theatrical text is built from a series of semicircles. The number of semicircles depends on the playwright much as the number of Acts in an Aristotelian structure is varied from one playwright to another or from one theatre movement to another. What is necessary is to describe what each semicircle contains structurally. Before the first compression begins, every play begins with an **exposition** which is characterised by:

---

[4] Figure 2 was drawn by Ethan-John Stoffels based on my hand drawn sketches.

- Drumming/music/dancing
- *Sarungano*/narrator giving an expose of the story
- *Ngonjera*/chorus/bards sharing the expose of the story
- Duologue that does the function of 2 and 3
- A creative combination of any of the above.

In the exposition, the main characters are introduced including those that will join the story later by way of mentioning them and what they will deliver to the problem just exposed.

A movement that is executed through semicircles is called *kuzvongonyoka*/sidewinding. When it is executed horizontally it leaves a track on the ground called *mwezva* in Shona. When this movement is executed vertically as in a human climbing a tree, it is called *gonyerebundu* in Shona. I am convinced that this term is derived from a type of caterpillar which moves by way of undulating movements which reach their climax by forming a loop in the middle followed by another forward thrust, another loop, in that order until it has reached its destination. I would call this formation, *mwezva*/concertina structure which can combine both horizontal and vertical undulating movements. When this movement is simulated in a computer, it produces a series of compressions with tensions at the top of the loop resulting in dislocation. Dislocation will lead to deformation of any material that is subjected to such force. The African play operates using the same principle. The first compression may be likened to what Brecht calls an episodic unit. In African plays written in English, Ama Ata Aidoo was the first to abandon the use of Acts and replacing the term with a more appropriate term, 'Phase', in the play, *Anowa* (1965). A Phase would be synonymous with Compression. Why is it a compression? Because the force is felt locally without causing the aftereffects to change the outcome of the next compression. The action is nearly self-contained causing the heat of the moment to circulate within the same area. In this compression, performers interact with one another and may engage in any manner of conflict which does not necessarily have a cause-and-effect schema. There could be song and dance, ceremonial cantos, and narration that may be full of spectacle. Because compression is a force that will be felt by the audience and performers, it results in a dislocation or state of quasi-stasis where the story/performance breathes. This quasi-stasis is characterised by:

- The arrival of a new performer, especially in *rombe* plays.
- The stalling of action to allow the narrator/*sarungano*/chorus/*ngonjera*/bards to enter the stage to give commentary on the story, other characters, and the major questions that need answers or to narrate the story.
- Ensemble singing, in which the song is an integral part of the narrative.

- Song and dance in which these codes are an integral part of the narrative.
- Moving scenery around (where it is used) for the next compression to take place.
- Or a creative combination of any of the above.

It is not a complete stasis, but a slowing down of the narrative to allow the audience to breath, experience aesthetic relief, and allow ideation to take place. From there, another undulating movement is initiated following the same schema as before. What is important to note is that this structure is not devoid of climax. By the end of the play, the audience/reader would have experienced multiple high moments or, in other words, mini-climaxes. In the Aristotelian structure, all linear movement is directed towards one major climax/explosion. Without a climax (anti-climax), the play would have failed. This structure is gendered male since it has a single climax which signals the end of the play as no more action can be pursued after the climax and denouement. In the concertina structure, all the compressions are enjoyed even without a climax, they can produce multiple climaxes, and for that reason, the structure is gendered female. The source of pleasure is melody and spectacle.

Dariro/Canto

Most African plays do not use 'scenes' in constructing a narrative. The term 'scene' raises certain expectations which are not always satisfied in an African play, especially of the *rombic* genre. In the western sense, a scene is an action which takes place at the same place in continuous time. It involves a set of characters who see the same issue in different ways leading to sustained dramatic action as they pursue their goals. A scene is therefore a play in miniature and should have the qualities of a dramatic play with a beginning, middle, and end arranged in a Freytag pyramid structure displaying a clear setup, turning points/payoffs, emotional transitions, and choice. The characters involved have clear goals, execute dramatic action, conflict ensues and is intensified on the basis of willpower of characters or one of them which reveals their values and personal traits (see Thomas, 1992, pp. 65–90). Not all of these qualities of a scene can be found in a *rombic* play or even the African epic theatre. In fact, several southern African languages deploy terms that deviate from the western scene. Shona uses *dariro* which translates to 'circular play-ground', Zulu uses *indawo* which translates to 'a place', Xhosa uses *umbuniso* which translates to 'the showing', while Tswana uses *lefelo* which has the same translation as the Zulu word for scene. Conceptually, in Africa, a scene is seen and experienced differently from the western one. It is at once a place of showing, seeing, and a playground. In the historiography of performance in Africa, what is seen or watched is not some fictional story existing in a fictive world but it is part of reality. That is why the performers are not called actors. Actors play fictional characters and live in a fictional world. The performers are called players, and they live in real time. Therefore, the place of seeing and playing is occupied by players as evidenced by the words used in African languages to describe them; *umdlali* (Zulu), *mutambi* (Shona), *Modiragatsi* (Tswana), *sebapadi* (Sotho), and *moraloke* (Pedi) all meaning 'player' and not actor. The same words are used for athletes, soccer players, or gamers. Indeed, Efua Sutherland in her play, *The Marriage of Anansewa* (1975), uses the word 'player' as a designation for what western theatre would call an 'actor'. She is the first to canonise the word in English in an official published play, although of course plays written in African languages have used it before her. For Africans, stage performance and playing are described by the same word which means they are similar. Therefore, the African scene played by players/ performers cannot possibly be the same as the western scene played by actors.

Because of its uniqueness to African (and possibly Asian and Latin American) performance, I want to call this second smallest unit after the Act, a *dariro*. The closest in meaning to this word is the Latin 'cantus' meaning song which when pronounced in English is canto. Canto entered the British Encyclopaedia in 1911 to describe a special type of poetry which was sung by the minstrel. In today's language, a minstrel is a performer/entertainer skilled in gaming, singing, juggling, acrobatics, and so on. All these activities align with what African performers do in the *dariro* which does not require them to be fully developed three-dimensional characters realised only by actors. The term is preferable for its nonconformity, anti-structure, non-plot based, and fragmentation. When used in English poems, it carries the same qualities of being part of a poem which can stand on its own. It helps to divide a long poem into individual sections (not to be confused with stanzas which are much shorter) and is of irregular length. Epics also use cantos as major building blocks.

Why do I use the term canto as a translation of *dariro*? Because it fully captures the essence of an African *dariro*. Gcina Mhlophe's *Have You Seen Zandile* is made up of fourteen cantos, although the playwright calls them scenes. They do not necessarily read as scenes because none of them leads to the next scene in a logical way following the cause-to-effect principle. They are standalone stories, some of them with little to no conflict at all. The only constant in all these cantos is the character, Zandile, playing with her grandmother or friends and discussing matters relating to growing up as a girl/woman. All the fourteen stories are different and independent of others; they don't develop a coherent plot built on the basis of a Freytag pyramid structure. The structure is circular. I would liken cantos to bees in a hive. All of them are drawn into shape by the presence of a queen bee. The queen in *Have You Seen Zandile* is the telling of women's stories. The stories can stand independent of each other, but they stick together through the force of thematic cohesion – the plight of Black women growing up in an apartheid state.

In Andrew Whaley's rombe play, *The Rise and shine of comrade Fiasco*, the play is made up of a single compression which is built on seven cantos. While in Mshengu Kavanagh's *Katshaa* the cantos are written down by the author, in Whaley's play, they can be discovered through reading. The play involves four performers who are thrown into prison for public violence. While in prison, they play seven games, none of them assisting the other story. What makes the games cohere is their preoccupation to find out if Comrade Fiasco was a legitimate ex-freedom fighter or a fake.

The last part of the structure is deformation. I name it so because all the effort of performers, which causes the action to meander around, does not result in a finished fully formed structure. The 'anti-structure' mantra of colonialist criticism emanated from this quality of African performance, as they wanted the structure to reproduce the Aristotelian one. If anything, the compressions and dislocations cause deformation at the end. The endings are normally disruptive rather than resolution. All *rombic* plays end disruptively without resolution. Epic plays end by suggesting another possible compression. The destination has not been reached despite experiencing wobbling/undulating/serpentine movements. Since the ending cannot be fully planned and fixed, the play is de-formed at the end, in a positive way. Unlike western absurd theatre which attacks story (*fabula*) in favour of discontinuity, psychic automatism, games, dislocation of language, and demystification of reason, *rombic* theatre is centred around an intelligible story which, however, does not obey the dramatic structure. It is made up of at least one compression and a series of cantos. Each of the cantos makes sense on its own but is not inclined to assist other cantos in developing the story. The *fabula* is truncated making any attempt at imposing absurdist theory problematic as some of the tenets of the theatrical text will not lend themselves to the schema. The usual judgemental comment 'the play has failed at being fully absurd' will be preferred by western critics in the absence of an African theory of the *rombic* theatre type, and thus this contribution. In western absurd theatre, the characters are mysterious, often without a past and advance atheistic existentialism. In *rombic* theatre, the characters have a past and the source of their suffering is often revealed by the playwrights.

4 Afrosonic Mime: A Post-psychophysical Perspective

This section proposes the performatic technique that I call the Afro-technique as a departure from psychophysical perspectives. I have defined Afroscenology as including two major components: the theory of the performer as the Afro-technique and the theory of the playtext as theatric theory. In this section, I will theorise on one tenet of the Afro-technique called Afrosonic mime. While the technique was observed occurring as tacit knowledge in several African productions across Zimbabwe and South Africa, my examples will be drawn from several laboratory performances at the University of the Witwatersrand, Johannesburg. I teach the course, Performance Practice, under the rubric 'African Aesthetic' as one of three performer training lecturers who run the two-year course Performance Practice in the Department of Theatre and Performance. During the first semester at first-year level, students develop a performance from a presentational play belonging to what we refer to as the 'African great tradition'. At second-year level, students devise their own work deploying this Afro-technique. I analyse these examples to discuss how Afrosonic mime makes the invisible visible. While discussing this tenet of Afroscenology, I seek to re-language the practice and develop critical vocabulary to share the technique with scholars across the global north and south.

Contextualising Afrosonic Mime

Afrosonic mime is one of the theoretical tenets of Afroscenology. Since both the theory and its tenet are new, I want to explain both and their historical origins. Afroscenology is an extension of Molefe Asante's Afrocentricity in the field of theatre and performance as outlined in Section 1. Afroscenology is a theory located in African theatre and performance which fulfils that role. The term is constructed from the root word of Africa and that of scenery respectively to create the neologism, Afroscenology. It is preoccupied with the study of African scenes/stories/theatre created by Africans and Africanists for purposes of performance to create a new language of description. It is hoped that this new language of description will assist in a better critique of African theatre which, for many years, has depended on theory manufactured in the West. The danger of deploying western theory in African theatre is that western theory was not developed through observing African theatre practices, but practices that were obtained in their specific contexts. The danger is that African theatre will be judged based on values drawn from elsewhere invariably leading to production of poor imitations of western practices or, in the worst-case scenario, finding faulty African performances where they refuse to follow western theoretical constructs.

Afroscenology is therefore a method of African performer training of creating African theatrical texts and a theory of critiquing. Both the method and the theory are derived from the practice drawn from the African 'great tradition' developed by practitioner-scholars who entered the academy from the moment of decolonisation beginning with Ghana in 1957. These practices soon found resonance with theatre companies which earlier on had been involved in struggle theatre. The techniques developed during this phase became the bedrock upon which the new post-liberation theatre was established. It is from these practices that Afroscenology is constructed. Afroscenology is therefore an Afriway of writing, performing, training, creating, and conceptualising these processes. As part of developing the terminology for this theory, I want to focus on one of the tenets which I have called Afrosonic mime.

Given the complicated history of the African continent which has seen part of its identity moulded by colonialism, slavery, Christianity, Islam, and other transnational influences, the construction of this theory is not a regression into an isolated nativistic approach; it is a reflection of everything that makes up contemporary African performance. The beauty of the theatre practice from which this theory is constructed is that it cannot be found anywhere in the world except in Africa and parts of its diaspora. For that reason, it deserves an identity of its own encapsulated in the term, Afroscenology. Just like structuralism provides a norm for understanding and talking about the structure of texts, words, units of texts, performance and design or realism provides rules for creating a constructed reality, Afroscenology provides norms, standards, rules, values or in short, a language to create and critique African playtexts, performances, designs, choreography, writing, voice, and directing derived from the African canon itself. The practice already exists as tacit knowledge. This section turns tacit knowledge into explicit knowledge by providing the concepts and vocabulary to read the work.

So, what is Afrosonic mime? I use the term to refer to a type of mime deployed by African performers when they reproduce physical action which signals an absent referent, whatever the signified may be, for example, an object, a prop, a boundary, a force, feeling, or whatever shape the referent may take. All cultures can mime, but they do not possess the same language to express that which is mimed. Thus, Lecoqian, Artaudian, and Grotowskian mime differ significantly from Afrosonic mime. While in western mime, music is normally deployed, especially in pantomime, to accompany what is mimed through the hands and facial grimaces, in Afrosonic mime, musical amplification is not part of the embodiment, but performers mobilise a soundscape produced by their vocal instruments. This soundscape, except in special circumstances, reproduces the sound of the referent under similar conditions of the action being mimed. If it is a bomb explosion, opening of door, knocking, cooking, and so on, the performers who enact the action realistically produce the sound of the action by the voices. While music in western mime or any culture is experienced viscerally rather than intellectually, it causes a semiotic problem in the sense that it is an icon which shares little to no connection with its signified.

It is simply an emotional experience. In an African presentational or postrealist play/performance which deploys a soundscape produced by the live human body, with a few possible exceptions, the sound refers to something that is already known in human memory. I therefore use the term Afrosonic mime to designate it as a separate but related practice. Afrosonic is a compound word formed from Afro- which links the practice to the geopolitical space of Africa. The prefix is combined with sonic to suggest that the practice depends on the deployment of vocal aural elements as means of signification.

I am not trying to create a separate artform as has happened in France and possibly several other western countries where mime has been weaned off from dialogue theatre. I isolate the theoretical tenet of the Afro-technique to explain it. I want to make sense of it by deploying a concept first conceived by Gilles Deleuze and Felix Guattari (2013) and developed further by Manuel DeLanda (2016) called assemblage theory. Indeed, the decolonisation of theory by manufacturing new theory from the global south does not necessarily mean the rejection of western theory or philosophy. As correctly noted by Nigam (2020, p. 29), decolonisation is simply 'treating it (western theory) as one among the many sources of thinking – that is to say, we must think across traditions'. Nigam goes on to make a fundamental observation on which my use of assemblage theory is predicated. He asserts that, 'At its most fundamental level then, theoretical decolonisation is about standing on our feet and thinking for ourselves – drawing resources for that thought like intellectual bricoleurs, from all manner of sources. That is what theory and philosophy were always meant to help us do.'(2020, p. 29)

In explaining the functioning of Afrosonic mime, I do so through articulating it with a concept that already exists which speaks to interconnectedness of elements. Indeed, Afrosonic mime can be understood in relation to other elements which contribute to its constitution. Before the concept was translated to English as 'assemblage', the French coiners of the concept called it '*agence-ment*' which speaks to the process of fitting and matching together and the outcome of such action. However, when the creators of the concept, Gilles Deleuze and Felix Guattari (2013), started explaining it and linking it to separate aspects of their philosophy, it started developing multiple meanings to a point where the different definitions could no longer be reduced to a single coherent notion. However, for purposes of establishing a working ethos, assemblage is defined as

> A multiplicity which is made of many heterogenous terms, and which establishes liaisons, relations between them, across ages, sexes and reigns – different natures. Thus, the assemblage's only unity is that of a co-functioning. It is a symbiosis,

a 'sympathy'. It never filiations which are important, but alliances, alloys, these are not successions, line of descent, but contagions, epidemics, the wind. (DeLanda, 2016, p. 1)

Assemblages are not restricted to material objects but many other elements which may be intangible. The theatre, in general, is made up of assemblages of the cast, set design, lighting, sound, and costume designs. In the case of African presentational or postrealist plays, the performance itself is made up of the spoken word (dialogue/text), dance, mime, and, song, all supported by a robust design of set, costume, and lighting. Theatre by its very nature is an assemblage of various constituent elements and their linkage in creating meaning. Frank Camilleri has made an interesting observation on what he calls 'dynamic hybrids' (2019, p. 91) to refer to non-human organisms and objects as part of sociality. When these non-human agents are deployed in theatre, they participate in the meaning-making process and take on the role of actors. Relying on earlier work by Greimas, Camilleri calls these human and non-human agents, 'actants', arguing that they are intertwined in conditions of hybridity. Because the term actor and its derivative 'actant' are problematic in describing African postrealist theatre, I prefer to use the terms, 'performer' (*mutambi/umdlali*) and 'performants' (*zvitambiso*), to describe similar relationships. In applying the concept of assemblage to theatre, Camilleri extends the possibility of linkages beyond material objects (materialities) to include the world of thoughts, imaginations, conventions, ideologies, and so on. These immaterial entities affect and equally contribute to the constitution of the material world. In the case of realist/ naturalist theatre, there is a tendency to ignore the immaterial (invisible) and focus on the material (visible) performants in analysis. While all other performants of the assemblage are important in explaining the concept, what is of interest to me in discussing Afrosonic mime is the assemblage of the human agent (performer) and what she/he imagines. The other immaterialities, like ideology, epistemology, axiological codes, non-aesthetic codes, regulators of behaviour, ethics genre, school of thought, aesthetic movements, and so on, would be irrelevant in this section. The imagined is performed as if it is present and therefore takes the role of a non-human performant creating a dynamic hybrid with the human performer.

It is this articulation between the performer and the imagined object which shapes the manner of Afrosonic mime. The greatest tool in realising the mime is imagination. The imagination produces the image of the non-human performant and places it in the theatre space and allows the human agent to navigate around the imagined performant. I call this 'imagistic imagination'. In realist/naturalist theatre, the material world is represented by material objects which imitate those in reality. The stage then activates everything which is put on it with signifying power which they lack in reality. In African postrealist theatre, non-human performants do not normally have a physical presence. It is the human performants that bring the non-human performants into existence through imagination. In the hands of a gifted performer, the imagined world with all its materialities such as doors, windows, oceans, rivers, chairs, corridors, etc. will be made visible by way of mime. The performance seen by the audience will be experienced through representation of those things in the mind and their manipulation in their absence. The image created in the mind is played by the body in such a way that the referent will be clear to the audience. While Stanislavsky required a certain level of imagination to actualise the given circumstances, he was assisted by the presence of set pieces on stage. In the African sense, a hyper-imagination is required as most of the things would be absent.

Mime is meant to overcome the limitations of the medium of theatre in conveying material reality. In the case of Afrosonic mime, it has developed specific conventions which I will be theorising hereafter. I will be answering the following questions:

- How does Afrosonic mime overcome the limitations of the medium of theatre in conveying information of the material reality?
- How does Afrosonic mime overcome the limitations of the medium of theatre in conveying information/activities that are taking place in the mind of the character or in a human organ such as a stomach, vagina, penis, and so on?
- How does mime overcome the limitations of the medium of theatre in present-ing machines on stage like a helicopter, a bomb blast, an aeroplane, and so on, or vast expanses of geographical spaces like a sea, a river, and so on?
- How does mime overcome the limitations of the medium of theatre in shifting from one location to another?
- How does mime overcome the limitations of budget?

Vectorisation

Before I talk about the different mime techniques found in Afrosonic mime, I want to dwell on the process of creating mime which also speaks to cultural legibility. Since this is a new performance technique, at least its theorisation, it will be important to establish the process of gathering vectors/fragments and provide typography which may be useful in increasing legibility. This is import-ant in intercultural performances such as Afrosonic mime. Vectorisation is a method or concept that is used in linguistics, computer science, mathematics, physics, genetics, and pathology. Perhaps the list could be larger. I would like to borrow this concept from these fields into the field of theatre and performance as a way of explaining different techniques used in linking different components of the story being told. Most African postrealist playscripts/performances are non-linear and, in some cases, anti-narrative. They are made up of several compressions and multiple micro-compressions that have a semicircular structure. These compressions always end with a deformation before another compression begins. Miming sequences dissolve into each other creating new sequences. In Afrosonic mime, the creative collective always provides mechanisms to allow the audience to follow the story. I have called the meaning-bearing components of the story vectors/*zvipenga* (Shona). Vectorisation is a technique of linking fragments/*zvipenga* together to form larger and multiple units of meaning(s). The closest Shona phrase to describe vectorisation is *kubatanidza zvipenga*. In computer science, vectorisation enables problems to be solved efficiently reducing the chances of error. In genetics, vectorisation happens where there is cloning from a host/vector when a piece of data-bearing tissue (DNA) is inserted into another host's cell to solve a genetic problem. It appears in both its scientific and artistic usage, vectorisation is intended to solve a problem by joining at least two components containing a set of data.

The first process is that of gathering, accumulating, or compiling. Some of the accumulators predate a performance, for example, dances, songs, games, and techniques which are all contained in the playing culture or general text of the group. These are units already encoded with meaning. Some of the materials will be created in the rehearsal space through improvisations/etudes. Afrosonic mime does not have an established sign language and the practice, and its meaning must be negotiated during the rehearsal process. What remains constant, however, is the use of aural codes which accompany a physical action which is mimed. These practices of gathering are named *vunganidzo/buthela* in Shona and Zulu, respectively. They have a similar definition to the English word, accumulators. It is these accumulators that will require other techniques such as connectors/*shanganiso/izixhumi* (Shona and Zulu, respectively). When the story uses flashback, for example, performers have a set of techniques to take their audience into the past. While doing Dambudzo Marechera's *The Alley* in 2017, performers executed a fast-track backpedalling accompanied by a rewinding sound. To come back to the present, they performed a similar technique. My second-year students doing *Kwapalwalwa* deployed a technique of turning around on the same axis ending with a verbal clue, '19 years later'. Again, there is no single convention; there are several ways of doing so.

It is not at all times that connectors will be supplied by the performers. Sometimes they just shift from the one sequence to another arbitrarily.

This technique is overdetermined in postmodernist plays where it is called discontinuity. I borrow the term syntagmatic gap from linguistics which denotes a relationship between two or more units. This relationship will be produced by the audience after seeing at least two sequences arbitrarily joined. Syntagmatic gaps are anti-narrative, but when used together with connectors, there will be narrative legibility. Perspectivals are a set of vectors which carry ideological meanings. They are sometimes called shifters or drivers/*muchairo/gazvo* (Shona). When a shifter or driver is used in its herding context, it is a violent metaphor which suggests whipping to keep the herd in the required direction. In the context of machines, it is a respectable image which suggests a steering wheel (*gazvo*) to keep the vehicle in the intended direction. The Afrosonic technique is not pursued for simply an aesthetic end. Aesthetic practices serve as resources for political work. Postmodernism furthers an ideology which dismantles metanarratives and their insistence on truth creating a post-truth world. Afroscenology promotes Africa and Africans. This is where the technique connects with Afrocentricity, especially its preoccupation with liberation and telling stories from Africa using Africa as a strong place to stand on. All the aforementioned vectors and the way they are connected must lead to a consensual ideology which allows Africans to play agential roles that promote and protect their personhood. Hereafter, I focus on how Afrosonic mime overcomes the limitations of the medium of theatre by way of new conventions.

Realistic Mime

To illustrate the notion of realistic mime, I want to refer to a workshopped piece by my second Performance Practice 2 students called *Kwapalwalwa*. This is a story about a family headed by a single mother, MaJobe, with four girls and one boy. The mother opens the story by calling her children in song and they immediately enter the stage with much singing and dancing. They are all wearing scarves on their necks and use black pants as costumes to indicate that the body is neutral and will be a vehicle to play different personas and inanimate objects. MaJobe introduces herself and the story, and suddenly the children lower their voices while continuing the playful dancing to give room for the mother's voice to be heard. As she speaks, she uses realistic mime/representational mime or in Shona, *kuyedzesera kwezvok-wadi*. The loose translation of the Shona phrase is truthful mime. Through realistic miming, she lays clothes on the imaginary line, picking them from the imagined laundry basket. When she is done with hanging the clothes, she mimes holding the laundry basket and walks offstage. The children then take turns to introduce themselves and their hierarchy in the family. There is a moment of transition where all create a kinetic tableau of a van. They produce its erratic starting sound shaking like its body. They produce its engine noise as they begin to move around the stage. Simultaneously they shift between producing the noise of the car and playing human passengers. All this is produced in a single human machine shaking, moving, and talking, all at the same time. The scarves are still around their necks.

This technique of realistic mime can be deployed in a published play. First-year Performance Practice 1 students rely on any published African postrealist play. I want to refer to the first compression of Andrew Whaley's play, *The Rise and Shine of Comrade Fiasco*, which was chosen by my students. They decided to give it a working title, *Ukuvula*. The characters are in a bar called Musongosongo. At this stage, all of them are patrons. There is no built set to establish the location. Bodies moving in space will soon define the boundaries and the set pieces. Music is blurring in the bar, but the soundscape is produced by human voices as the players dance in the space to the tune of their own musical voices. The different spaces in a bar must be established. One of the performers is standing behind a counter which he mimes and opens a bottle of liquor by miming the action. The imagined bottle becomes a performant as it causes a series of other actions. On opening the bottle by miming the action, the performer also produces the fizzling sound of the drink. Suddenly two patrons move towards the counter to order drinks for themselves. They do so while both chatting and dancing to the music they produce by their mouths. The bartender delivers the order by miming and handing over the imaginary glasses. He opens another bottle of beer and the bottle top pops out splashing the contents on the male patron. The sound of the popping and splashing is produced by the performers. This provokes a fight. The victim, Sithina, grabs the bartender by the collar. There is no physical touching; he simply grabs the air and the bartender, in sympathy to the action, moves as if he is experiencing the force exerted on him. The Zulu language uses the phrase, *ukudlala ngomoya*, to describe realistic mime. The loose translation of this term is 'playing with air'. Performers create meaning by performing actions in the air in the absence of referents that are being mimed. As the bartender is 'fished' out of the cubicle, the physical boundaries established earlier are respected. The beating follows the same convention. Sithina punches the air and the other patrons in the bar experience the pain by responding by screaming and jumping. Patrons act like one choral body to amplify the action being mimed.

Kinetic Tableau

Tableaux are already known in theatre as denoting a picture of a scene with storytelling qualities in which one or more persons are positioned in striking ways, sometimes with props and scenery. They combine aspects of theatre and visual arts. Derived from the French term *tableau vivant*, meaning 'living picture', tableaux are often used by street performers who pose as statues in public spaces. This concept of a living picture can be extended to the theory of Afroscenology to explain a mime variation used by African performers. Whereas a tableau is normally a frozen picture, the liveness of theatre can convert the still images into kinetic images to overcome the limitation of the theatre medium in portraying material reality such as machines, cars, animals, and nature. Shona has a word that describes this phenomenon. A photograph is called *mufananidzo*. When we add motion (*famba*) to the word, we end up with a neologism to name a kinetic tableau, *mufananidzofamba*, which loosely translates to moving image(s). Based on the last example in *The Rise and Shine of Comrade Fiasco* of a fight in the bar, I want to demonstrate how kinetic tableau works. While the fight is going on in the bar through a miming process as just described, there is a moment of transition indicated by a caesura and then all bodies in the bar dissolve from their participation in commotion to a single file to mime the dispatching of a police vehicle to neutralise the fighters in then bar. One plays the police siren, another uses hands to mime the flashing of police lights, and others produce the sound of the engine, all playing the varied actions simultaneously; one cannot pick which one is doing which activity. This tableau of human bodies moves towards the area earlier marked as a bar. The kinetic tableau comes to a stop and the different parts of the police vehicle dissolve into police officers. The performers don't cerebrally become a police car, all the actions are exteriorised thus breaking the psychophysical ethos of character conception.

I want to return to the workshopped performance, *Kwapalwalwa,* to explain further the workings of kinetic tableau. Picking up from the story of MaJobe who has left the stage miming holding a laundry basket, the next transition reveals MaJobe coming back to the stage, but this time having shoved her scarf into her black shirt to project her as pregnant. She sits down in the delivery position and begins to make some noise associated with labour. The rest of the players dissolve the van tableau and quickly construct another one of a vagina. The scarfs are now used as sculpting material to establish the labia and pubic hair. But, like most African kinetic tableaux, the performants are not restricted to one role of establishing the vagina, but they join in the choral chants of inspiring MaJobe to push to deliver the baby. As the mother cries in agony, the movement of the vagina is magnified in the kinetic tableau. With more move-ments of the constructed vagina, the baby, played by one of the performers, somersaults out of the opening. MaJobe removes the scarf from her belly and holds it in her hands like she is already a baby. The constructed vagina dissolves and quickly forms another tableau of a gate leading to a *sangoma*/shaman's sacred space. One of the performers disengages from the group and crosses the gate threshold as a *sangoma*, but now using her scarf as *ishoba* or tufted cow tail used to wave away curses and to sprinkle medicine on patients. MaJobe crosses the same threshold to seek counsel from the *sangoma*. The *sangoma* gets possessed by a spirit and performers dissolve the gate tableau and form a screen board on which the spiritual experiences of the *sangoma* will be projected. Whatever happens within the *sangoma* is given expression by this kinetic tableau of performers sometimes in abstract movements. When the consultation comes to an end, the performers dissolve the screen board tableau and revert back to the gate tableau through which both the *sangoma* and MaJobe exit. At this stage, performers have transitioned into several personas and non-human performants; they have not maintained one character as would be the case in a typical Lecoq mime performance.

Psychomages/*Fungiramumoyo*

This is a neologism from psyche and images. In other words, it captures what is happening in the mind or other internal spaces in the body such as intestines, urethra, and so on. The Shona equivalent is *fungiramumoyo*. The ancient Shona thought that the heart was the one doing the thinking as all emotions were experienced in the heart. They have a figurative expression called *fungiramumoyo rwendo rweimbwa* which literally means that a dog knows its destination by way of moving to it but is incapable of explaining it. However, in the case of psychomages, what is thought or experienced in the mind or internal organs is given expression through mime. In my MA creative project, *Trauma Centre* (2001) performed at the University of Cape Town, I had three deranged characters, Reito, Zeppelin, and Themba, isolated in a mental hospital. In one of the bizarre scenes, one of the characters, Zeppelin, mimes masturbating. As he reaches orgasm and releases his sperms, one of the characters, Themba, performs a sperm as he travels through the urethra racing with other millions of sperms to go and fertilise an ovule. At the moment of escaping the penis, the sperm and others suddenly realise that it is a dead end. They fall to the ground and die. The sperm persona dissolves and returns to playing Themba, the deranged patient.

Somewhat related to *psychomages* are what Jacques Lecoq calls *mimages*. In Lecoqian terms, *mimages* are gestures used to express the state of being of characters, in short, their emotions. In filmic language, these would be 'close-up shots' to view how emotions play themselves on the face of the character by zooming in on the surface of the face. The facial skin becomes a stage on which movements of the skin and what it excretes in response to an intense feeling will be magnified. However, in the language of mime, these emotions are expressed through *mimages* to dramatise the internal turmoil of a character. I have expanded the scope of *mimages* to include spiritual visitations in characters which are then played out by a choral collective to express in abstract movements the impact of the spirit on the host character. In 2017, I directed Dambudzo Marechera's *The Alley*. In one of the compressions, one of the characters, Robin, remembers his evil deeds while serving in the Rhodesian army. Through performing a connector (quick backpedalling to the sound of a rewind sound) to the past, he is seen interrogating and torturing a Black woman, Cecilia Rhodes. He asks her to sing 'God bless Africa' as he unzips his trousers in preparation to rape her. In the moment of lapse of concentration on the part of Robin, Cecilia snatches a pistol from Robin's loins and fires a shot at him. He ducks and escapes, but another soldier rushes in to finish off Cecilia. He shoots her but not before she fires at him. They both die. At remembering this moment, Robin's mind experiences post-traumatic disorders and imagines Cecilia and the soldier resurrecting as demons and moving to attack him. The spirits are played out by the Cecilia and the soldier in abstract movements which suggest menacing and vengeance. Robin discovers a cross lying on one of the benches and uses it to attack the demons. The cross performs miraculous powers which send the demons scampering for cover. This energy radiated by the cross is felt and expressed in movements which I have called *spirimages*. *Spirimages* disregard the laws of nature and will be expressed in weird and ethereal style. The *mimage* ends, and there is momentary darkness accompanied by music. There is costume change is to reconnect with the previous sequence of external reality and not this one of the spirit and psychological world.

Conception of Space Deploying Afrosonic Mime

In Western theatre, there are two dominant forms of stage space. Christopher Balme calls the first 'successional stage' (2008, p. 55). This created space represents the objective reality and all action invariably takes place on the same location. As is the case with this use of space, shifts of time and place will be indicated through exits and entrances of characters. The second type is what Balme calls the 'simultaneous stage' (2008, p. 55). Instead of one location, the space is divided into several locations which act in a similar manner as the successional space. The action of the play will alternate these locations. Both these spaces are mimetic, meaning that they are created by the designer as icons to imitate reality. Where the theatre as an artform has failed to produce such similarity, it creates a convention to compensate for the imitations, e.g., mimetic paintings to represent huge icons like oceans, mountains, rivers, and so on.

Scenography and visual art assist in creating these spaces. These spaces are empty containers waiting to be filled but they are objective concrete spaces marked by their tangibility. Pavis uses the term 'centripetal space' to refer to these dominant western spaces. This is a term he borrows from physics where a centripetal force moves from the periphery (petals) towards the centre. The space is framed, and attention is focused from the peripheral end to the individuals occupying the framed space. Nothing is extended beyond what is framed except through diegetic means like description of offstage space by a performer or use of recorded sound to suggest something outside what the audience can possibly see on stage.

In the context of Afroscenology, space is conceived in a different way. While the performance may take place in a constructed theatrical space with a stage space (whatever form it may take) and liminal space which separates the audience from the performers, the performance space/*dariro* (Shona) will not have the qualities of either a successional or simultaneous staging. Granted, performers (*vatambi/abadlali*) may use a couple of props, but these will invariably not maintain the same significance. The sign will transform into other uses and meanings as just discussed relating to the scarf. To resort to the physics metaphor, the African space in an African postrealist play will be centrifugal. Centrifugal is the opposite of centripetal. The force extends from the centre radiating outwards. It is the bodies of performers occupying the space which extend and contract the space according to the conditions dictated by the performance. Describing this space, Pavis (2003) asserts that 'it is conceived as invisible, unlimited, linked to its users, determined by their coordinates, movements and trajectory; space as a substance not to be filled, but expanded and extended' (2003, p. 150). This Afroscenological space has some qualities of what semioticians call diegetic space. Diegetic space is not seen by the audience but is described or referred to by characters in the play. Similarly, Afroscenological space cannot be seen; it is described by bodily gestures and suggested by aural codes produced by performers. If successional and simultaneous spaces can be perceived, the opposite is true for Afroscenological space. It can only be conceived in the mind and not perceived. I refer to the performance of *The Rise and Shine of Comrade Fiasco* by some of my first-year students. They chose the second compression of the play which they titled *The Search*. The second compression comprises the search for Comrade Fiasco. This is a game played by prisoners after their arrest at Musongosongo Bar. They are now in prison, but they expand the space of their prison cell through moving in the space and creating new spaces. From the prison cell, they begin to tell stories about themselves. This story involves a vigilante group that takes it upon itself to search for a person who raids their village at night in search of food. It is the story of Fiasco himself and how he ended up in this cell where the story is being told. Everything is done without the aid of props or costumes. All players/performers wear black pants.

The first task is to establish the locale of the story which is a mountain with its flora and fauna. How does mime overcome the limitations of theatre to present a mountain on stage? The alleged criminal, Fiasco, is hiding in a cave on this mountain. He is visible to the audience but is invisible to the performers who will soon establish the rules of the space through their bodies moving in space. Two performers can be seen on stage. They are not playing human, but inanimate performants by swaying here and there and producing the sound of the wind vocally. The swaying of bodies on their own may not be interpreted correctly but when accompanied by sounds, the mental picture is completed. It is difficult for an audience member to miss the meaning when a gifted performer embodies an object with a sonic aid. Soon three vigilantes appear on the stage. They obey a certain set of rules – the space is bushy, thorny, and potentially dangerous. As they move on this space, they effect their movements guided by the rules of the space. The absent thorns and bushes are made visible through the performer's bodies as they move in the space tiptoeing and stealthily. The three vigilantes add more adjuvants (helpers)/*mumera/mmela* (Shona and Zulu, respectively) to increase believability of space as a mountain. They produce the sounds of birds and animals associated with the mountain. A combination of these various sounds creates the appropriate ambience. They mime carrying pistols and torches. These vigilantes cannot be characters; they are players/performers oscillating between man, animals, birds, and wind. This has to be maintained for believability. As they reach the opening of the cave (its size has not yet been tested), they begin to pick up clues. The first clue is a footprint, and they argue over it. The next one is an empty tin of condensed milk. It is mimed, picked, and poked with a finger to collect the remnants. All three vigilantes taste the contents through mime. They treasure the sweetness of the milk and then disperse in different directions pointing their torch beams (mimed) in the direction they are moving. The second vigilante notices a cave opening, kneels down to establish the size of the opening, and directs a ray of light inside the cave. At this stage, the cave is only marked by a body and an opening which has just been established. Its depth and length are not known until the space is activated by bodies moving in it. The second vigilante calls others and they obey the original size of the opening established earlier on. All three direct their rays (mimed) into the cave. They now add more adjuvants (*mmela*) to activate the space. As they enter the cave, they crawl into it establishing the diameter of the entrance. As soon as they enter the space, they figure out that they can stand in it. The next step is to establish its expanse and as they arrest Fiasco, they restrict their movements to the limits of the cave marking its entire area. Afrosonic mime has successfully constructed a mountain in the imagination of the audience and above that has managed to create a space within this space – a cave, without the aid of any design elements.

As soon as Fiasco has been arrested and pulled out of the cave, all three vigilantes and two players performing trees start miming descending a mountain. The two players performing trees transition to parents holding a school meeting and they are joined by the second vigilante. This meeting is interrupted by two vigilantes who now display Fiasco at the meeting as the criminal who terrorised the villagers at night. The meeting dissolves, and all six players transform to a chorus/*ngonjera* (Swahili) and offer commentary about Fiasco and his evil deeds as they move around him in coordinated choreography. Incensed by this public humiliation, Fiasco snatches a pistol from one of the vigilantes and charges at all of them. He is subdued and suddenly the commotion dissolves and the chorus reconstitutes itself as a police vehicle into which everybody will participate as a kinetic tableau to get to the police station. The players return to their original role of prisoners but play the next game of being police officers.

5 Conclusion

Afroscenology has three dimensions to it, the theory of the text which I call the theatric theory to distinguish it from the Aristotelian dramatic theory. Related to this theatric theory is the narratology theory which explicates the processes of telling African stories through dialogue, stage directions, and other extra-textual elements (*performativesness*) generally called codes of content or epistemic codes. The third component is the performatic theory which explains and re-languages the African technique of performance/acting. This Element was only able to pick one of the genres of African theatrical texts, *rombic* theatre, to demonstrate the theatric theory. This theatric theory is not only applicable to *rombic* theatre, but most African plays which refuse to toe the realist tradition. The performatic and narratology theories will be subjects for different studies. While the performatic theory or what I will call the Afro-technique has nearly nine tenets– hyper-imagination, Afrosonic mime, vectorisation, kinetic tableau, bifurcation, organicity, spirituality, physical action, and etudes – this Element has picked only one tenet, Afrosonic mime, and explained how it works. The other topics not covered in this Element will be subjects for other works.

In delineating the theory of Afroscenology, I have used what Michael Etherton refers to as the African 'great tradition' or 'art theatre' (1982, p. 24) and my own practice as a performer/actor trainer and director. These terms refer to plays that are written down by African intellectuals and professional theatre-makers to form an African canon from which a theory can be established. My theory is based on experimental works that were developed in laboratories pursuing the noble goals of developing African theatre such as arts researchers who experimented using university resources like Wole Soyinka, Ngugi wa Thiong'o, Hussein Ebrahim, Robert Kavanagh Mshengu, John Clarke, and Ola Rotimi. I also relied on the great tradition developed by township theatre innovators who refused to regurgitate old western plays but created their own new works like Cont Mhlanga, Mbongeni Ngema, Percy Mtwa, John Kani, and Gibson Kente who sometimes worked with white liberals like Christopher Hurst, Barney Simon, and Athol Fugard. Here African playwrights/theatre-makers were beginning to experiment with form and content, creating predom-inantly African works. While transnational influences may not be ruled out, they play a supportive role rather than dominance. The earliest forms began in the 1930s with Herbert Dhlomo, lapsed and re-emerged in the 1960s during the first phase of political decolonisation when the first African countries were gaining their independence.

In the African humanities and in theatre and performance, in particular, scholars have been very successful in developing a language of critiquing coloniality. Regrettably no alternative theories and methodologies have emerged to replace or counter the ones they critique. A cursory view of the most recent literature about decolonisation will confirm this anomaly, Ndlovu-Gatsheni's *Decolonisation, Development and Knowledge in Africa* (2020), Nigam's *Decolonzing Theory* (2020), Smith's *Decolonizing Methodologies* (2021), Jansen's *Decolonization in Universities* (2019), and even earlier philo-sophical work like wa Thiong'o's *Decolonizing the Mind* (1987). In other fields, there will be many more works on decolonisation. Yet, despite this tremendous output on critiquing coloniality, scholars still deploy or repurpose theories and methods developed in the West to process raw data collected in African contexts. This situation does not change the unequal power in the academy. There is a need, especially in theatre and performance, to break out of this colonial mode of intellectual production which, according to Nigam, requires the establishment of 'our own manufactories, our own infrastructure where the business of knowledge production can take place' (2020, p. 12). The fact of the matter is that we need to change theory by creating new ones that emerge from our local practices. As we do so, new vocabularies, concepts, categories of thought, and frameworks will emerge when we re-language our practices and methods. It is comforting to note that, in Southern Africa, a different brand of theatre has been emerging since the era of liberation struggles. Many play-wrights like Fatima Dike, Gcina Mhlophe, Athol Fugard (for some of his plays),

Kabwe Kasoma, George Mujajati, Dambudzo Marechera, Percy Mtwa, Mbongeni Ngema, and Barney Simon have been producing work through individual effort or a workshop/devising process creating work that borrows techniques from struggle theatre and the general text/playing culture found in townships and rural communities. In contemporary South Africa, younger theatre-makers like Prince Lamla, Monageng Mtshabi, Mandla Mbothwe, and Zimkhitha Kumbuca, to mention a few, continue to advance this kind of theatre. The works created do not resemble any works produced anywhere in the world. It is unique to Southern Africa with comparable examples in West Africa. Some of the works such as *Woza Albert* have gone on to win awards in the USA confirming their robustness and innovation. The question remains, where is the training which emerged from this unique practice? Is there a regime of knowledge which can be systemised into a technique to enable the rest of the world to benefit from it? If theory comes from practice, where is the theory that emerged from this work? This Element has partially answered some of these questions and subsequent volumes will fully answer all of them.

A question may be posed, with Africa's diversity, can there be a theory for the African continent? We now know from the work of Raymond Williams (1977) that 'a structure of feeling' that grips a generation causes human actors present in the period to create work in ways that are invariably similar to respond to the troubles and joys of the time. Thus, in Africa and the diaspora, there was work that at once aped Western models out of pressure from colonial discourse which had discredited all African artistic endeavours as primitive and superstitious. There was a time that Africans and the diaspora created work around the concept of Negritude to respond to the reawakening African spirit after the failure of integrative assimilationism. There was a time when most of the Black creatives chose to speak to their fellow Black audiences about being proud of their blackness and deploying techniques culled from the African general text such as rituals, ceremonies, songs, dances, and mime under the banner of Black Power and Black Consciousness Movements in America and South Africa, respectively. These movements produced Black Art which despite geographical differences exuded similar techniques. There was a time that Africans resident on the African continent decided to take up arms against colonial masters and war generation artists responded by creating struggle/combat theatre deploying similar techniques in most African countries. What these examples serve to demonstrate is the fact that, with a few possible exceptions, a structure of feeling may cause human actors to produce artistic works which respond to their pressures in similar ways without having held a conference to agree on a style. Since theory comes from practice, there can be a theory that scholars can develop to explain practice.

Will this theory work for all African practice? Throughout the history of theoretical propounding, there has not been a single theory that works for all art and a geopolitical space. While realism was taking root in the West, young creatives were beginning to problematise it by creating work which deviated from the norm; expressionism in Germany, futurism in Italy, and surrealism in France, all of which brought forth the theory of modernism. Similarly, Afroscenology was developed to cater for African work that emerged soon after independence. Most African governments caused the formation of drama/theatre departments soon after independence to assist in the reconstruction of the defamed African image. Scholar-practitioners like Wole Soyinka, Efua Sutherland, Ama Ata Aidoo, Hussein Ebrahim, Stephen Chifunyise, Ngugi wa Thiong'o, Kabwe Kasoma, and a few white collaborators like Michael Etherton, Robert Mshengu Kavanagh, Malcolm Purkey, Athol Fugard, Martin Banham, and Peggy Harper started developing plays and performances which advanced decolonisation. At the same time, professional theatre companies that were independent and/or affiliated to universities emerged which developed the same style of plays. The theatre-makers who come to mind are Cont Mhlanga, Dambudzo Marechera, Athol Fugard, John Kani, Percy Mtwa, Mbongeni Ngema, Barney Simon, Ben Abdallah, Ngugi wa Mirii, Gibson Kente, and many others. The work of these scholar – practitioners and professional theatre-makers suggests a particular style from which the theory of Afroscenology is developed. It is a theory developed from specific examples located in Africa and more specifically, Zimbabwe and South Africa. My reading of Ngugi wa Thiong'o's *Decolonising the Mind* (1987), Sam Ukala's *Politics of Aesthetics* (2001), and Awo Mana Asiedu's *Abibigoro: Mohammed Abdallah's Search for an African Aesthetic in Theatre* (2011) suggests that this theory will find resonance in West Africa and East Africa where some of the work mentioned aforementioned was developed. I have not sufficiently studied theatre of the Maghreb and Horn of Africa to make any claims about the applicability of this theory in those contexts. Other scholars may develop different theories to cater for those environments. Difference may be articulated in a different theory. Just like those who were unhappy with realism developed modernism and postmodernism in the western world, those unhappy with Afroscenology may propound post-Afroscenology or, however, they may wish to coin the terminology.

Does Afroscenology mean destroying bridges and building a secluded African particularism? Does it mean jettisoning theories and practices from the West and other regions? Certainly not. It is desirable that we, in the Global South, break the colonial mode of knowledge production where the

Global North harvests data as is the case in economics where raw materials are sourced from the south to be processed in the North and sold to the South, at a premium, as processed finished products. In the case of knowledge, the North returns theory for Africa to use with tremendous cost to the South's knowledge economy. What I am proposing here is what Nigam calls 'import-substituting theorisation' (2020, p. 18). This allows African scholars to think of their present independently. Epistemic independence, however, does not mean rejecting western theory; it means that it remains as one of the pathways of thinking or what Nigam calls our ability to 'think across traditions' (2020, p. 29) and 'drawing resources for that thought like intellectual bricoleurs, from all manner of resources' (2020, p. 29). It will be noted that, in reaching some of my conclusions, I relied on western theory.

To date, many books on African theatre have been written. James Currey is the most invested publisher of African theatre and has today published nineteen volumes of themed African theatre books. There have been several others on African theatre history, performance analysis, dramatic literature, drama therapy, applied theatre, and some such topics. No single book or journal article on African theatre has proposed a theory of African theatre. This Element breaks new ground by propounding the theory of Afroscenology. This Element may contribute to re-languaging and systematising the African theatre. Universities the world over are presently preoccupied with the decolonial project. While the theatre practices mentioned in this Element may already be evident and known in teaching laboratories and various theatre companies, there are no intellectual tools available for their formal teaching in the classroom. The default position is to rely on techniques that are recorded in books like the Stanislavskian psycho-technique, Alexander technique, Mesner technique, Vhaktangov technique, and Chekhov technique which advance western hegemony in theatre training.

From the experience of Molefe Asante's construction of the theory of Afrocentricity, the work has the potential to provoke debate among scholars causing further academic explosions resulting in works formed around the controversy. The Element will potentially cause a stir. Regions which feel left out will race for new theory and methods. Those who feel threatened by Africa's contribution to theory will respond as was the case with Asante's Afrocentricity. Those who agree with my findings will apply the theory in their respective fields and cause more intellectual work to be produced. The Element's major contribution is to break the cycle of academic whining and complaint against coloniality by propounding a theory which challenges Western theories of acting, dramatic text and performance.

This Element serves as a kind of introduction or treatise on the theory of Afroscenology. In the current form of this Element, part of the Afroscenology theory captured here will be useful for script analysis for performers and directors, script writers, writing students, their teachers, and theatre critics. All theatre directors and performers working on a pre-written script begin the process with a thorough engagement with the text trying to understand the foundations of plot, the environment, the backstory, narrative progression, structure, (non)character, thought/idea/meaning, narratology, tempo-rhythm and style (see Thomas, 1992; Catron, 1989; Knopf, 2017). To understand these elements, available western theory veers towards Aristotelian elements, making it difficult to fully understand African playtexts, most of which are differently constructed into semicircular structures, neither always producing miniature Freytag pyramid structures nor sustained conflict, causing further explosions, and intensifying towards a climax. What this Element offers is the creation of new categories of analysis and renaming them. Where the western-oriented director focused on thought/idea/meaning and how the performance should be organised to convey the meaning/knowledge, this Element takes this issue as assumed knowledge and gives the director/performer a second dimension not entirely dependent on the word/logos. This is the dimension of mime, song, dance, poetry, action, visual dramaturgy, or in short, *performativeness*, and how these can be organised to create not just meaning but an atmosphere, an orientation, or spectacle of sorts.

To the playwrighting student and teacher, a play is no longer exclusively understood in terms of the dramatic structure – exposition, rising action, climax, denouement, and resolution; work can be developed using different structural elements such as expositions, compressions, cantos, discontinuities, and deformations. The new building blocks can sideline dialogue as the dominant feature. This may entail song, dance, mime, poetry, reportage, and dialogue. As such the Element suggests a different model of structure and could be used to develop decolonised assessment criteria for performance, writing, and analysis. To the theatre critic, a different lens has been provided to critique post-linearity, (non)characters, stories, structures and performance. I hope that the need to conform to the ethos of dramatic theatre has been problematised through suggesting an alternative approach. The world has many theatres with equally different approaches to making, writing, performing, assessment, and critiquing. This Element is Africa's contribution to a better understanding of theatres of the world, specifically African theatre of the type explained in this Element.

The penultimate Section 4 hopefully has engaged with the performatic theory which will be useful in actor/performer training. The approach of this section is not 'how to'. That can be done in a textbook on performer training. Theory by its very nature is an abstract description of the relationship between ideas, statements, and concepts which help us to understand the world. I hope that Section 4 has deepened our understanding of African performance through a description of one of the major pillars of African performance – mime, named here, Afrosonic mime. Follow-up works will certainly complete the descriptions.

References

Achebe, A. 1975. *Morning yet on creation day*. London: Anchor Press.

Acholonu, C. O. 1984. 'A touch of the absurd: Soyinka and Beckett', in E. Jones (ed.), *African Literature Today*, 14, pp. 12–18.

Aidoo, A. A. 1965. *The dilemma of a ghost and Anowa*. New York: Longman.

Amuta, C. 1989. *The theory of African literature: Implications for practical criticism*. London: Zed Books.

Asante, M. K. 1987. *The Afrocentric idea*. Philadelphia: Temple University Press.

Asante, M. K. 2007. *An Afrocentric manifesto: Toward an African renaissance*. Cambridge: Polity Press.

Asiedu, A. M. 2011. 'Abibigoro: Mohamed Ben Abdallah's search for an African aesthetic in the theatre', in Kene Igweonu (ed.), *Trends in twenty-first century African theatre and performance*. New York: Rodopi, pp. 367–384.

Balme, C. 1999. *Decolonising the stage: Theatrical syncretism and post-colonial drama*. Oxford: Clarendon Press.

Balme, C. 2008. The *Cambridge introduction to theatre studies*. Cambridge: Cambridge University Press.

Biko, S. 2004. *I write what I like: Selected writings*. Johannesburg: Picardo Africa.

Bradley, F. Brown, K. & Nairne, A. eds. 2001. *Trauma*. London: Hayward Gallery Publishing.

Camilleri, F. 2019. *Performer training reconfigured: Post-psychological perspectives for the twenty-first century*. London: Methuen Drama.

Carlson, M. 2003. *The haunted stage: Theatre as memory machine*. Ann Arbor: University of Michigan Press.

Catron, L. E. 1989. *The director's vision: Play direction from analysis to production*. Mountain View: Mayfield Publishing Company.

Chifunyise, S. 1986. 'Dance Drama', in Bulawayo Workshop, Ngũgĩ wa Mĩriĩ, and Zimbabwe Foundation for Education with Production (eds.), *Community based theatre skills: Report of Bulawayo Workshop, 19–20 July 1986*. Harare: ZIMFEP, pp. 35–40.

Chifunyise, S. 1997. 'Foreword', in Robert Mshengu Kavanagh, *Making people's theatre*. Johannesburg: Witwatersrand University Press, pp. i–ii .

Chifunyise, S. and Kavanagh, R. M., eds. 1988. *Zimbabwe Theatre Report*, No.1. Harare: University of Zimbabwe Publications.

Chinweizu, C., Jemie, O & Madubuike, I. 1980. *Toward the decolonization of African literature: African fiction and poetry and their critics*. Enugu: Fourth Dimension Publisher.

Chinyowa, K. C. 2007. 'Towards an aesthetic theory of African popular theatre'. *South African Theatre Journal*, 21(1), pp. 12–30.

Chinyowa, K. C. 2015. 'Play as an aesthetic discourse in African cultural performances'. *Contemporary Theatre Review*, 25(4), pp. 534–544.

Clarke, J. P. 1966. *Ozidi*. Oxford: Oxford University Press.

Coplan, D. 1987. 'Dialectics of tradition in South African black popular theatre'. *Critical Arts*, 4(3), pp. 5–27.

Couzens, T. 1985. The New African. A Study of the Life and Work of H. I. E. Dhlomo. Johannesburg: Ravan Press.

Crossley, J. 2017. The cyber-guitar system: A study in technologically enabled performance practice. Unpublished doctoral thesis, Wits University library, Johannesburg.

De Marinis, M. 1993. *The semiotics of performance*. Indianapolis: Indiana University Press.

DeLanda, M. 2016. *Assemblage theory*. Edinburgh: Edinburgh Press.

Deleuze, G. & Guattari, F. 2013. *A thousand plateaus: Capitalism and schizo-phrenia*. London: Bloomsbury.

Davhula, M. J. 2015. Malombo musical arts in Vhavenda indigenous healing practices. Unpublished PhD thesis, University of Pretoria library, Pretoria.

Dhlomo, H. I. E. 1939. 'Nature and variety of tribal drama'. *Bantu Studies*, 13(1), pp. 33–48.

Dhlomo, H. I. E. 1977. 'Drama and the Africa'. *English in Africa*, 4(2), pp. 3–8.

Dhlomo, H. I. E., Visser, N., & Couzens, T. 1985. *H.I.E. Dhlomo collected works*. Johannesburg: Ravan Press.

Ebewo, P. 2008. 'Holding talks: Ola Rotimi and theatre of the absurd'. *Marang: Journal of Language and Literature*, 18, pp. 153–160.

Elam, K. 1980. *The semiotics of theatre and drama*. New York: Methuen.

Etherton, M. 1982. *The development of African drama*. New York: Africana Publishing Company.

Fanon, F. 1963a. *The wretched of the earth*. London: Penguin Books.

Fanon, F. 1963b. *The wretched of the earth*, Farrington Constance (transl.). London: Penguin Books.

Fleishman, M. 2012. 'The difference of performance as research'. *Theatre Research International*, 37(1), pp. 28–37. https://doi.org/10.1017/S0307883 311000745.

Foot-Newton, L. 2005. *Tshepang: The third testament*. London: Oberon Books.

Foucault, M. 1980. *Power/Knowledge: Selected interviews and other writings, 1972–1977*. New York: Vintage.

Fourie, P. J. 1988. *Aspects of film and television communication*. Cape Town: Juta.

Fugard, A. 1972. 'Sizwe Bansi is dead', in *Township plays*. Oxford: Oxford University Press.

Fugard, A. 1983. *Boesman and Lena*. Oxford: Oxford University Press.

Gwala, M. 1973. 'Towards a national theatre'. *South African Outlook*, 103, pp. 131–133.

Goffman, E. 1974. *Frame analysis: An essay on the organization of experience*. Middlesex: Penguin Books.

Hamutyinei, M. 1973. *Sungai Mbabvu*. Gwelo: Mambo Press.

Hauptfleisch, T. 2005. 'Artistic outputs, arts research and the rating of the theatre practitioner as researcher – Some responses to the NRF rating system after the first three years'. *South African Theatre Journal*, 19(1), pp. 8–34. https://doi.org/10.1080/10137548.2005.9687799.

Kavanagh, R. M. 1985. *Theatre and cultural struggle in South Africa*. London: Zed Books.

Kavanagh, R. M. 1997a. *Making people's theatre*. Harare: University of Zimbabwe Press.

Kavanagh, R. M. 1997b. '*Mavambo*/First steps'. In R. M. Kavanagh (ed.), *Making people's theatre*. Harare: University of Zimbabwe Press, pp. 189–227.

Kavanagh, R. M. 2016a. *Selected plays 1: The theatre of workshop '71*. Harare: Mshengu Publications.

Kavanagh, R. M. 2016b. *Making theatre*. Harare: Themba Books.

Kavanagh, R. M. 2017. 'Katshaa', in *Selected plays II: The political theatre of Zambuko/Izibuko*. Harare: Mshengu Publications.

Kavanagh, R. M. 2019. Hamba Kahle MK. Unpublished play workshopped with Wits Theatre and Performance students at Wits Theatre.

Kavanagh, R. M. 2022. 'Realism, non-realism and the African performer'. *South African Theatre Journal*, 35(1), pp. 36–44.

Kaviraj, S. 2009. 'Marxism in Translation: Critical reflections on Indian radical thought', in R. Bourke and R. Guess (eds.), *Political Judgement: Essays for John Dunne* . Cambridge: Cambridge University Press, pp. 172–199.

Keir, E. 1993. *The semiotics of theatre and drama*. London: Routledge.

Knopf, R. 2017. *Script analysis for theatre: Tools for interpretation, collaboration and production*. London: Methuen.

Marechera, D. 1994a. 'Killwatch', in *Scrapiron blues*. Harare: Baobab Books.

Marechera, D. 1994b. 'The alley', in *Scrapiron blues*. Harare: Baobab Books.

Mazrui, A. 2009. 'The seven biases of Eurocentrism: A diagnostic introduction', in R. Kanth (ed.), *The challenge of Eurocentrism: Global perspectives, policy and prospects*. New York: Palgrave Macmillan, pp. xi–xix.

Mbembe, A. 2017. *Critique of black reason*, Laurent Dubois (transl.). Johannesburg: Wits University Press.

Mda, Z. 1993. *We shall sing for the fatherland*. Johannesburg: Ravan Press.

Meyer-Dinkgräfe, D. 2001. *Approaches to acting: Past and present*. London: Continuum.

Mhlanga, C. 1992. *Workshop Negative*. Harare: College Press.

Mhlophe, G. 2002. *Have you seen Zandile?* Durban: University of KwaZulu Natal Press.

Midlands State University (MSU). 2010. Ordinance 5. Unpublished university ordinance on staffing and promotion, Gweru.

Mtwa, P., Ngema, M., & Simon, B. 1983. *Woza Albert*. London: Bloomsbury Methuen Drama.

Mutambara, A. 2014. *The rebel in me: A ZANLA guerrilla commander in the Rhodesian bush war, 1975–1980*. Solihull: Helion and Company.

Mutwa, C. 1981. 'uNosilimela', in R. M. Kavanagh (ed.), *South African people's plays*. London: Heinemann, pp. 1–61.

Nigam, A. 2020. *Decolonising theory: Thinking across traditions*. New Delhi: Bloomsbury.

Pavis, P. 2003. *Analyzing performance: Theatre, dance and film*, D. Williams (transl.). Ann Arbor: University of Michigan Press.

Pradier, J. M. 1995. 'Ethnoscenology manifesto'. *Theatre/Public*, 123, pp. 46–48.

Ravengai, S. 2001. Trauma centre. Unpublished play in MA thesis, University of Cape Town Library, Cape Town.

Ravengai, S. 2002. Thoughts that think in straight lines cannot see round corners: Transgressing the realist narrative form. Unpublished MA dissertation, University of Cape Town library, Cape Town.

Ravengai, S. 2011. 'The dilemma of the African body as a site of performance in the context of western training', in K. Igweonu (ed.), *Trends in twenty-first century African theatre and performance*. Amsterdam: Rodopi, pp. 35–60.

Ravengai, S. 2018. 'Decolonising theatre: Subverting the western dramaturgical frame in Zimbabwean theatre and performance'. *Critical Arts*, 32(2), pp. 15–30.

Rotimi, O. 1979. *Holding talks*. Oxford: Oxford University Press.

Sauter, W. 2008. *Eventness*. Stockholm: Stockholm University.

Schechner, R. 1988. *Performance theory*. London: Routledge.

Smith, L. T. 2021. *Decolonising methodologies: Research and indigenous peoples*. New York: Zed Books.

Solberg, R. 1999. *Alternative theatre in South Africa: Talks with prime movers since the 1970s*. Pietermaritzburg: Hadeda Books.

Soyinka, W. 1964a. The strong breed. In *Three short plays*. Harare: College Press, pp. 79–120.

Soyinka, W. 1964b. The swamp dwellers. In *Three short plays*. Harare: College Press, pp. 1–42.

Soyinka, W. 1965. *The road*. London: Oxford University Press.

Soyinka, W. 1971. *Madmen and specialists*. London: Methuen.

Soyinka, W. 1976. *Myth. Literature and the African world*. Cambridge: Cambridge University Press.

Sutherland, E. 1975. *The marriage of Anansewa: A storytelling drama*. California: Longman Press.

Taylor, P. C. 2016. *Black is beautiful: A philosophy of black aesthetics*. West Sussex: John Wiley and Sons.

Thomas, J. 1992. *Script analysis for actors, directors and designers*. London: Focal Press.

Turner, V. 1988. *The anthropology of performance*. New York: PAJ Publications.

Udenta, O. U. 1993. *Revolutionary aesthetics and the African literary process*. Enugu: Fourth Dimension.

Ukala, S. 1996. 'Folkism: Towards a national principle for Nigerian dramaturgy'. *New Theatre Quarterly*, 12(47), pp. 279–287.

Ukala, S. 2001. 'Politics of Aesthetics', in Banham M., Gibbs, J. and Osofisan, F. (eds.), *African Theatre: Playwrights and Politics*. Oxford: James Currey, pp. 29–41.

Wa Thiong'o, N. 1987. *Decolonising the mind: The politics of language in African literature*. Harare: Zimbabwe Publishing House.

Wa Thiong'o. N. 1993. *Moving the centre: The struggle for cultural freedom*. Oxford: James Currey.

Wa Thiong'o, N. (adaptation by Kgafela Magogodi & Prince Lamla). 2018. *Devil on the cross*. New York: Penguin Books.

Wa Thiong'o, N. & wa Mirii, N. 1982. *I will marry when I want*. Johannesburg: Heinemann.

Whaley, A. 1991. *The rise and shine of Comrade Fiasco*. Harare: Anvil Press.

Whitmore, J. 1994. *Directing postmodern theater: Shaping signification in performance*. Ann Arbor, MI: University of Michigan Press.

Williams, R. 1977. *Marxism and literature*. Oxford: Oxford University Press.

About the Author

Samuel Ravengai is Associate Professor and former Head of Department of Theatre and Performance at the University of the Witwatersrand, Johannesburg, South Africa. He is currently the Assistant Dean of Graduate Studies in the Faculty of Humanities at Wits University. He holds a PhD and MA in Theatre and Performance, both from the University of Cape Town. He is particularly interested in the interconnection of race, nation, empire, migration, and ethnicity with cultural production. Ravengai's most recent publications are *Theatre from Rhodesia to Zimbabwe* (2021) published by Palgrave Macmillan, a book chapter in *The Palgrave Handbook of Theatre and Migration* (2023), and an article in *South African Theatre Journal* 33(1) 2020 published by Taylor and Francis. He is currently involved in the research project called Afroscenology which seeks to propound and document a theory on African and Diasporic aesthetics based on their practice across several years. He is on the Editorial Boards of *Performance Ethos: An International Journal of Ethics in Theatre and Performance*, *Imbizo: International Journal of African Literary and Comparative Studies,* Palgrave Book Series: *Performance and Migration* and is Editor of *South African Theatre Journal* (Routledge).

Acknowledgements

My obsession with decolonising African theatre began in the 1990s with an honours research report grappling with the redefinition of African theatre arguing for a separate practice which is not an overseas extension of western theatre. The inspiration came from the University of Zimbabwe English Department, especially from a course called Language and Literature taught, at the time, by Dr Muzi Mlambo. Many thanks to you. Many thanks to Professor Kole Omotoso who examined my master's dissertation at the University of Cape Town and during the *viva voce* pushed me to create African terms for *rombic* theatre that I had just directed as part of my creative practice. The seed that was planted in that moment has grown and is explained in this Element. Rest in Peace Professor!

At the University of the Witwatersrand, I pay homage to the *Fallists* who shook the corridors of power through the *#Rhodesmustfall* and *#Feesmustfall movements* and gave impetus to the decolonisation agenda which had been unfolding at a snail space. A special thank you to colleagues at Wits Theatre for supporting the creative work we do from which some of the ideas registered in this Element emerged and for permission to use photographs in this Element. Thank you to my students, especially those who participate in my creative works which provide empirical data to some of my conclusions and to the cohort which joins the Afroscenology Research Project. They teach me a lot about African theatre through their research and gifts in the many South Africa languages.

Thank you to Kundai Ravengai with whom I have built a life for the past twenty-five years outside my professional and creative life.

I dedicate this Element to five African theatre-makers, Stephen J. Chifunyise who perished in 2019, Kennedy C. Chinyowa who left us in 2021, Sam Ukala who departed in 2021, Cont Mhlanga who passed on in 2022, and Ama Ata Aidoo who was promoted to glory in 2023. All these African giants dedicated their lives to decolonising African theatre through creative practice and/or theorisation. Playwrights do not die; they live forever through their ideas and works. Rest easy great creatives of Africa.

Cambridge Elements ≡

Theatre, Performance and the Political

Trish Reid
University of Reading

Trish Reid is Professor of Theatre and Performance and Head of the School of Arts and Communication Design at the University of Reading. She is the author of *The Theatre of Anthony Neilson* (2017), *Theatre & Scotland* (2013), *Theatre and Performance in Contemporary Scotland* (2024) and co-editor of the *Routledge Companion to Twentieth-Century British Theatre* (2024).

Liz Tomlin
University of Glasgow

Liz Tomlin is Professor of Theatre and Performance at the University of Glasgow. Monographs include *Acts and Apparitions: Discourses on the Real in Performance Practice and Theory* (2013) and *Political Dramaturgies and Theatre Spectatorship: Provocations for Change* (2019). She edited *British Theatre Companies 1995–2014* (2015) and was the writer and co-director with Point Blank Theatre from 1999–2009.

About the Series
Elements in Theatre, Performance and the Political showcases ground-breaking research that responds urgently and critically to the defining political concerns, and approaches, of our time. International in scope, the series engages with diverse performance histories and intellectual traditions, contesting established histories and providing new critical perspectives.

Cambridge Elements ☰

Theatre, Performance and the Political

Elements in the Series

Theatre Revivals for the Anthropocene
Patrick Lonergan

Re-imagining Independence in Contemporary Greek Theatre and Performance
Philip Hager

Performing Nationalism in Russia
Yana Meerzon

Crisis Theatre and The Living Newspaper
Sarah Jane Mullan and Sarah Bartley

Utpal Dutt and Political Theatre in Postcolonial India
Mallarika Sinha Roy

Decolonising African Theatre
Samuel Ravengai

A full series listing is available at: www.cambridge.org/ETPP

Printed in the United States
by Baker & Taylor Publisher Services